T0117206

# THE RANDOM
# SERIES

# THE RANDOM
# SERIES

## RAJA VUDATALA

PARTRIDGE
A Penguin Random House Company

**To order additional copies of this book, contact**
Partridge India
000 800 10062 62
orders.india@partridgepublishing.com

www.partridgepublishing.com/india

# Contents

# Current Affairs

# Beyond Enemy Lines

## <u>13 *Monday* Oct 2014</u>

I think, Government of India lost a huge opportunity in altering the India-Kashmir-Pakistan narrative and national interest was again mortgaged to petty domestic politics. A stable and democratic Pakistan is as much a need for Pakistan as it is for India. Thus, efforts to strengthen Pakistan democracy should have been part of India's strategic thinking.

It is no secret that power in Pakistan is distributed among three elements, the Federal Government, the ISI and the Army. Off the three, the Federal Government has the least power and often struggles to prove its legitimacy, more so when it comes to international relations especially with India. However, **2013** saw for the first time a **democratically elected Government transfer powers to another democratically elected Government**. Given the history of military dictatorship in Pakistan, this was no mean achievement. So, in came **Nawaz Sharif** with a solid mandate. Nawaz Sharif has been known to be friendly towards India and in all his previous stints, as PM of Pakistan, he has made attempts to chart a new course in the Indo-Pak relationship. Needless to say the ISI-Army watches his steps closely for signs of weakness or softness in stand towards India. On the other side of the border, **2014** saw a first in the history of Indian democracy. For the first time in 30 years a single party got a complete majority in General Elections and first time since Independence a non-Congress party (BJP) came to power with a thumping majority. In came **Narendra Modi** with a solid mandate.

As a master stroke in Diplomacy, **Heads of state of all the SAARC countries were invited to the swearing in ceremony** of the new government. The invitation created a dilemma for Nawaz Sharif. If he rejected the invitation, the world would have said that the new Indian Government was attempting to thaw the relationship but obstinate Pakistan wasn't willing. If he accepted the invitation, people in Pakistan would have seen it as bowing down to India and India would have claimed victory. It is a known fact now that both the Army and Senior Journalists in Pakistan advised Nawaz Sharif against the visit, indicating that there isn't much to gain from the visit and Indians can't be trusted. It is also known now that Nawaz insisted and prevailed over all opposing opinions and decided to make the visit to India and attend the swearing in ceremony. For him, this was an opportunity to demonstrate legitimacy of the mandate, exert authority over the hawkish elements at home and show his seriousness towards economic development of Pakistan, through improved trade links with India. Two democratically elected Governments on either side of the border, with a significant mandate and a clear 5 year term ahead of them augured well for changing equations and relations. However, that wasn't to be and history repeated itself. A huge opportunity lost, probably for the whole of the coming five years.

Immediately after Nawaz Sharif's visit, Foreign Secretary level talks were to take place between the two countries. However, the meeting of Hurriyat Conference (HC) leaders with Pakistan's ambassador to India, was highlighted as an issue and the **Foreign Secretary level talks were called off**. For those in the know of these matters, HC leaders meeting Pakistan PM or Pakistan ambassador is a routine affair and has happened in the past. Although, the Pakistani Ambassador went ahead meeting HC leaders, the Pakistan PM however kept away from meeting HC leaders during his visit, thus signaling a friendlier stand. Yet, the meeting of HC leaders with Pakistani Ambassador was made into a serious issue and India refused to talk to Pakistan till such encouragement to separatist leaders was not stopped. Certainly this was a setback to Nawaz Sharif's strategy and strengthened the ISI-Army view point on India. It helped them to show what a mistake it was to have accepted the invitation to visit India, thus weakening the grip of Pakistan Federal Government on matters concerned with International Affairs.

Close on the heels of this incident came the August 14th 2014, **long-march in Pakistan**. With baseless allegations from Imran Khan of massive rigging during 2013 elections and call for revolution by Canadian based Tahir-ul-Qadri the future of Nawaz Sharif government became jeopardized. While the army was not willing to step-in and meddle into domestic matters they supported the protests that broke out in Lahore due to their dislike towards Nawaz. Mainly stemming from, attempts to try Pervez Musharraf and the recent drubbing by India. Faced with severe protests in Lahore/Islamabad/ Karachi and fast losing public support and a possiblity of his Government getting toppled, Nawaz Sharif brought up the issue of 'Plebiscite in Kashmir' at the UN General Assembly in September 2014. This, despite an agreement during Musharraf's regime that, plebiscite issue won't be brought up at the UNGA.

The trust deficit between the two Governments reached a new low!

**The floods in Kashmir** in September 2014, which many indicate to be a man-made disaster due to poor water resource management and ecological imbalance, gave a reason for the

Indian state to exert its legitimacy in J&K. The heroic activities of Indian Army during the relief work were highlighted time and again. However, it is known now that the relief activities were not fast enough and not sufficient enough and India turned down help offered by international community which would have helped to improve medical facilities required to prevent spreading of any epidemic. With the media no longer focusing on J&K flood victims, we don't know what their state is. However the message sent was very clear, that Indian Government run by BJP was in control of matters in J&K.

The other news doing the rounds was about the **ceasefire violations by Pakistan**. Interestingly, Indian media reported violations by Pakistan and Pakistan media reported violations by India, tough to know who's telling the truth. However, logic would say that with vast domestic unrest and the constant vigil required at the Pak-Afghan border, the army wouldn't like to open another front to worry about. Nonetheless, the reported intensity of ceasefire violations were so high that the Indian PM after speeches at Madison Square Garden, Dinner with Obama, election rallies in Maharashtra and loss of civilian life in the border area, decided to give a free hand to the Army to fire at will and destroy Pakistani posts. Now the Pakistani media is busy reporting heavy civilian casualty at their end and there are victory signs being flashed in India.

The trust deficit between the two Governments certainly hit another new low and might have reached a level from where reconciliation within coming 5 years becomes tough.

However, what certainly seems to be on track is **BJP's Mission 44+**. When viewed in the backdrop of Mission 44+ the Indian strategy becomes clearer and pieces of the puzzle tend to fall in place, albeit, it might have come at the expense of national interest. Proving that the BJP led Government is doing everything to help J&K and also extending all help through all resources at its disposal is a way to ensure that J&K people view BJP as the best option in the upcoming State Elections over PPP and NC and discrediting Hurriyat Conference completely. I certainly don't intend to say that everything Pakistan does is benign. I only want to point out that all that India does is not benign either. I also don't intend to point out that this is not the first time that domestic politics has influenced relationship with Pakistan or our stand on Kashmir. I only want to point out that the current Government is no different. Whatever be the outcome of the elections it is for sure that relations with Pakistan and hence legitimacy of Indian presence in J&K be settled amicably soon. More importantly the mandate at both sides has gone a begging.

# Judicial Profiling

## 06 *Monday* Oct 2014

The dissenting voice has become a rare commodity in today's India. The percentage of voter's turnout in the last election might have indicated a renewed belief in democracy and democratic principles. However, what has emerged in the aftermath has been quite different and disappointing. In all the mediums available there is bullying, bad mouthing, name calling and out shouting of any dissenting voice. Hero worship and blind faith has been at its peak. One would have hoped the elections were not mere symbolism but truly represented our commitment to democracy; however looks like our country might still not be ready for it.

The incumbent Government has certainly taken many positive steps and also giving indication of an economic revival and they are all welcome and certainly need to be appreciated. However wherever the Government has gone wrong it deserves to be criticized and must be criticized. The danger of hero worship and blind faith is the partisan view point that one takes of Government policies. This includes praising the good moves and ignoring the bad ones till the bad ones start hurting us more than the good moves manage to help us. It is this critique that is being choked and not being allowed to be heard over the din of hero worship. Personality cult is not new in India we have seen it in the past and we are seeing it again so not much has changed in the retrospect.

Are these misplaced apprehensions that I garner? I'll leave that to the reader to judge based on the facts that I present. There are 4 pillars on which Indian democracy stands. They are the Legislature, the Executive, the Judiciary and the Press. Even if one of these 4 pillars becomes weak the democracy might become a sham democracy. What I present here are ways in which the incumbent government has systematically weakened the pillar of judiciary.

**Using the ordinance route to appoint an ex-TRAI chief:** The Regulatory authority TRAI, was created to be totally independent of the executive, so that an impartial view on issues related to telecom could be provided. The independence of the authority was severely compromised when the Government got the ex-chief of TRAI, Nripendra Mishra, appointed as a Principle Secretary via the ordinance route. As per law minister Ravi Shankar Prasad, the ordinance merely corrects an anomaly that existed in the system. The anomaly that he speaks of is that of- any chief of such regulatory authorities not being eligible for posts in the Government even post retirement to ensure absolute independence. By going via the ordinance route the Government has ensured that successive chiefs of such regulatory authorities like SEBI or TRAI are mindful of possible post-retirement opportunities which could strongly influence their pre-retirement decision making. Purely on the strength of majority in the lower house and interesting floor management in the upper house, the ordinance was passed despite opposition from many quarters.

**Appointment of ex-CJI as Governor:** Close on the heels of the above decision came the decision of appointing ex-CJI as Governor of Kerala. Another instance where even the position of CJI has been compromised and its independence from the Executive, jeopardized. Even CJIs would be mindful of possible lucrative post-retirement jobs. So the judiciary has already been compromised. I won't even bring up the possibility of the ex-CJI being rewarded for favorably deciding on a case involving Amit Shah.

**Interference in appointment of Supreme Court Judges:** The incumbent Government interfered in and opposed the appointment of Gopal Subramanium as a Supreme Court Judge. The current CJI is on record expressing his anger and disappointment on how the current Government singled out Subramanium's name and objected to his candidatur. The matters were pushed to an extent where Subramanium was left with no choice but to withdraw his name from the list of applicants. This is sufficient to demonstrate the expanding powers of the executive without even having to bring out the point of the role Subramanium played as amicus curiae in Sohrabuddin fake encounter case related to 2002 Gujarat Riots.

**Not Allowing Leader of Opposition:** Power tends to corrupt and absolute power corrupts absolutely. Great men are almost always bad men' –Sir John Dalberg-Acton. The power of the Executive has been expanding as I indicate in the above instances and certainly has muscled its way on many instances in the Legislature too. For appropriate check and for a mature democracy like that of India certainly a leader of opposition is the need of the hour. Unfortunately the opposition is so fragmented that nobody automatically qualifies for the role. In the past Congress governments have been guilty of using their numbers to not allow leader of opposition. The current Government could have proved itself to be different by gracefully allowing the leader of opposition role to the single largest opposition party. Vinod Mehta, editor-in-chief of Outlook magazine, is on record saying that lets forget the past and also what the rule book says, it is essential for proper functioning of legislature that a leader of opposition be present to keep the Government in check. Despite repeated requests and discussions this request has fell on deaf ears and the speaker in LS has rejected it outright.

**Discarding Collegium system for appointment of Supreme Court Judges:** The collegium which used to appoint Supreme Court Judges was scrapped this year in favor of National Judicial Appointments Commission. It's interesting to note who the members of the NJAC are:

- Chief Justice of India (Chairperson, ex officio)
- Two other senior judges of the Supreme Court next to the Chief Justice of India – *ex officio*
- The Union Minister of Law and Justice, *ex-officio*
- Two eminent persons (to be nominated by a committee consisting of the Chief Justice of India, Prime Minister of India and the Leader of opposition in the Lok Sabha or where there is no such Leader of Opposition, then, the Leader of single largest Opposition Party in Lok Sabha), provided that of the two eminent persons, one person would be from the Scheduled Castes or Scheduled Tribes or OBC or minority communities or a woman. The eminent persons shall be nominated for a period of three years and shall not be eligible for re-nomination.

If the position of CJI is compromised by the Government; if the appointment of Supreme Court judges is influenced by the Government, if no Leader of Opposition is present what chances remain that the appointment made by NJAC would be fair and without influence of the Government? The independence of the judiciary, as I see it, has been permanently compromised.

The Executive is in expansionary mode, the legislature has suffered due to the muscle power of the executive and the judiciary is also reeling under the same weight. Thus, Modi's statement of *'Minimum Government and Maximum Governance'* is either not well understood or will only remain an eyewash.

# Party To It

Political parties are always in the middle of controversies yet they keep devising methods to steer clear of controversies. Looking at the number of controversies they keep getting embroiled in doesn't seem like they have managed to devise any successful methods.

I get particularly peeved when I see parties distancing themselves from statements made by members of their own party and terming such statements as '**individual opinion**' that the rest of the party doesn't endorse. This always seems to me to be the ultimate fraudulent, cover-up act that falls on its own face.

**What or who is a party**? A party is made by a group of individuals who collectively support an ideology or a purpose or an end objective. So it is made up of people with opinions and ideas. So, this group of people is the party and the party is the people. People evolve the party evolves and some ideas change and some disagreements also arise. The opinion of one individual cannot be considered to be the opinion of an entire party as then it is not a party but an individual with a group of followers and yet if it has to remain a party even individual opinions should be considered as party opinion

One might argue that there are so many party workers who support the party for reasons known best to them. How could the party take the responsibility of so many people coming from disparate background and with disparate objectives?

21

This somehow seems hypocritical that a party doesn't hesitate benefiting from the labor of a party worker but would not standby the same worker's opinions when expressed in public. Then the question arises how higher up in the **party hierarchy** should a party worker be for his opinion to be also considered as official party opinion? Obviously when opinions are expressed by party workers and it is worth air time on TV or space in the print media then it is somebody significant enough in the party hierarchy. Yet very conveniently parties distance themselves from anything said and not favored by media or larger section of people.

Parties might also argue that there is a **consensus opinion** and then there is an **individual opinion**. If party is formed by group of people with common ideology then either they shouldn't have differences of opinion or there should not be anything called a 'consensus opinion'. Even if one important member of the party has a different opinion then obviously consensus cannot be said to have emerged. Either the party should have discussed on all matters of importance and ensure each individual endorses the same opinion or refrain from talking in the public domain. However the truth is that the issues are so many and the world so dynamic that a party can't imagine meeting on all matters repeatedly or imagine for there to be a consensus on all matters. A party that can't accommodate differences of opinion can't stay a single unit for long.

Thus I conclude that **individual opinion is just as much a party opinion** as any. Infact as I indicate above there might not be anything called as a party opinion in most of the cases. So I think next time we hear any party distancing itself from statements made by any party member; we need to observe the individual in question, his seniority, the ulterior motive and decide for ourselves if really the party could distance itself from what is said or is it a double game the party intends to play!

# Battle of the Electorate

## 14 *Wednesday* May 2014

Elections 2014 are over and in a couple of days' time we would know who gets the people's mandate to govern the country for the next 5 years. Of course, if the public sentiment and the exit poll survey results are to be believed, we already know to some extent about who would be getting that chance.

We have had 15 such elections in the past and given opportunities to a party or to a group of parties to govern the country and take it in a path of peace, welfare, growth and prosperity. All of them have succeeded and failed simultaneously to varying degrees. Similarly, whoever emerges as the victor on 16th May 2014 would also succeed and fail like the Governments before them. Of course we do hope that the government succeeds more often than it fails thus making the 5 years tenure a net productive one.

What the party, that gets to govern, will do we will get to see it as it slowly assumes the role and executes its duty, I want to take the attention away from that point and move it what 'we the people' would do in the coming 5 years. The social media has been the battle ground for not only the political parties but for ordinary citizens like me, vociferously expressing our view points and justifying our stand and professing our support for one or the other party. Now that a particular party would be elected and be given the responsibility to govern, can all of we social media warriors or social activists go back to rest, knowing either we were successful in getting what we wanted or failed in our endeavor?

I think the need of the hour is for warriors like us to remain active and observe the journey that the elected government would take the country through and express our support or express our dissatisfaction on each twist and turn. The real truth is that it is not Modi's Sarkar or Rahul's Sarkar or BJP's Sarkar or Congress's Sarkar, it is **Our Government, Hamari Sarkar**, and it is answerable to us and only us. If we keep a constant, informed and politically literate vigil on the Government of the day – it would be forced to listen and work in a direction that is agreeable to most.

Of course we don't want leaders or parties that have to keep asking the people to make a decision for them; we do need a decisive government. Yet we need a Government that is responsive to the people apart from being accountable to the parliament. So to all my friends who spent hours on social media buttressing their view points, the time is now to be more active and take responsibility to ensure that we see a responsible Government that takes us in a direction that is beneficial to the whole country.

# League of Extraordinary Gentlemen

## 25 *Friday* Apr 2014

IPL -7 is well underway and already we have witnessed some very entertaining games. While I support no team and have no favorites, I do enjoy some sensational individual batting performances and sometimes good bowling performances. IPL, inspired by NBA or MLB format from the USA, was started in 2007. I won't discuss much about the history or inception of IPL as it could pretty well be read on Wikipedia. What I wanted to rather focus on was about the issue of betting and spot fixing that have marred the franchise and even threatened suspension of few teams or the tournament as a whole.

Even before stepping into IPL, probably we should start with understanding what BCCI is. BCCI is a private organization created out of the mutual consent of each of the State Cricket Boards, which are again a set of private bodies. It isn't a Government body nor is it Government funded. So in many ways what this means at the very outset is, it is neither answerable to the public nor is it responsible for the public. It's only objective is to take care the interest of the game and the players in the country.

Let's also look at the two oft used terms of **Betting and Fixing**. Firstly it is essential to distinguish and separate the two. Betting and Fixing are not essentially co-related. They could be mutually exclusive and have no interdependency at all. **Betting** is the idea of putting money behind a prediction, either that of a team winning or losing. While betting seems to be entirely based on a person's intuition, it is also aided with as much information as is available in the market. Some countries have legalized betting, pretty much like betting on horses; some countries still criminalize betting. Note that betting doesn't involve any interference with the result of a match. It is just about a person's intuition on what he thinks would be the outcome of the game and placing money on it.

**Fixing** on the other hand is about influencing a game towards a desired or pre-determined outcome for various benefits. This necessitates involvement of players and in extreme instances team management or umpires. Players could under-perform and umpires could give incorrect decisions. Needless to say that such acts of the player or umpires leads to huge monetary bonus. Sometimes fixing could be linked with betting. That is, if the odds are stacked against a particular outcome of any game then due to the vested interest of few the matches might be influenced deliberately.

Firstly it needs to be understood that legalizing betting would still leave the problem of Fixing un-fixed. Probably transparency in who is betting and what methods they deploy in the process might reduce their ability to influence outcome of games, but it might not be able to entirely rout it out. The question that arises now is even if a particular match is fixed should anybody be bothered? Let us think this through. **How we view betting depends on the country's legislation. If the legislation changes, betting becomes perfectly legal. What about fixing? I think fixing is a more complicated a matter**.

There could be many angles to look at the issue of match fixing. I will restrict myself to the point of view of the **audience or fans**. So there are a bunch of cricketers who want to play cricket, so there are teams formed who come together under an association. The association starts organizing tournaments where cricketers could showcase their talent and enjoy playing the game while competing against each other. So people get interested at what this association is doing and starts watching the games with interest. Soon spectators swell and they start selecting their favorite teams. The primary objective of the spectator is to be entertained and watch some good performance. Of course there is a matter of delight involved if ones favorite team wins. Imagine I as a supporter support Team A which is playing Team B tonight. I want Team A to win and go to watch the game between Team A and Team B hoping to be entertained and hope that Team A wins. Now some naughty players in Team A decide to under-perform due to the money they could make my being part of a match fixing process. So, Team A loses the match and I come away disappointed with the outcome. Even if I get to know that players in Team A deliberately underperformed for money, do I have a case against them? Is my disappointment a sufficient reason to have a case against them? As a fan of Team A am I not supposed to be mentally prepared for both victories and losses? As a fan I came to be entertained and I did get my entertainment.

Even a purist/pundit who wants to watch a game for the sake of fair play or keen competition doesn't have much to argue for. The game that was once played for 6 days in sunlight has come down to being played under light for just about 4 hours. Also many rules have been introduced to tilt the game in the favor of batsmen. So, anyway, a fan/audience is at the mercy of what is dished out, as the primary objective is entertainment. Entertainment is what we get whether the match is fixed or not and disappointment is what we get when the results are not in our favor. So fixed or un-fixed is more less one and the same from a viewer's standpoint. The association could also pretty well use the same argument. That, it is answerable only to the players and the players have been taken care of very well and it has made best facilities made available to press/media and audience through stadiums. It only charges a nominal charge from a fan to allow him to watch the match comfortably. Can it be held accountable for any betting or fixing issues even if there is one?

I think that the popularity of the game is definitely because of the audience who are devoting a significant amount of time, effort and money to watch these games with a hope of entertainment and a hope of delight to see their favorite team win. So as long as we are being entertained I think we don't have much to complain about. Or we have a choice, like WWF or what is called now a WWE, we can stop watching it all together!

# Why I voted for BJP

Elections in India have become one of the most vituperative, vindictive no holds barred competition between rival parties. The political calculations involved in deciding friends, allies or foes are mind boggling. Then there is a heady concoction of religion, caste, ethnicity and language that make the fight even more complicated for any analyst to say anything with confidence. In fact on innumerable occasion many psephologists and opinion poll surveyors have had to eat humble pie due to the Indian electorate proving them completely wrong.

I had to deal with my own dilemma prior to deciding who to vote for. All the parties that I considered had some factors going for them and many factors going against them. It became extremely tough to conclude who to vote for.

**Indian National Congress**: I would certainly like to believe that the India that I stay in now, has a large percentage of population that believes in earning a livelihood, credibility and respect through merit. Anyone appearing to be unduely taking advantage due to their birth is strongly detested. This India, I think, is disillusioned with the Congress party's enchantment with the Gandhi family. This time, certainly more than ever, the ship has decided to go down with the captain! The blatant arrogance with which the previous UPA2 Government went about with brazen acts of corruption and indifference has definitely not gone down well with anyone. Even the poorest of the poor who have been beneficiaries of some of the social schemes introduced by Congress, have shown their disenchantment with this party. A political party cannot drive the agenda of be a single family. This is outrageous and the party deserves to be in wilderness till the family and the party gets decoupled in some decisive way. Each generation of the family has been known to commit one major mistake that leaves some indelible mark in history. So I would definitely not vote for such a party.

**Aam Aadmi Party**: When the party was freshly formed in Dec 2012, I wrote about the chaotic nature of the party and how it appears to be a Hindi Belt party with socialism written all over it. Of course they pulled up a tremendous performance in the Delhi assembly elections surprising many; however a series of mistakes after coming to power has left me disenchanted with the party. There were lofty ideals but a bunch of disillusioned men/women whose only claim to idealism was the Aam Aadmi cap. The party also heavily depended upon one man, the man who the party needed so desperately to drive the Lok Sabha campaign that he had to beat a hasty retreat from the post of Delhi State's chief minister. What the hurry was I couldn't understand, what I did understand is that I can't vote them just as yet. I would like to see them work in the political sphere, gain knowledge, wisdom and organize their country wide cadre. Then I might want to re-look at their status by 2019 to decide if they get my vote or not. Though, I would also like to maintain that this party would continue to exert influence both in its success or failure. This is because, they would ensure other parties start becoming more transparent, focus on reducing criminalization and punish the corrupt without which, the big parties have started to realize that, even a new comer can beat them black and blue.

**Bharatiya Janata Party**: BJP and I have had a love hate relationship for a very long time. The history and origin of the party leave many questions unanswered. BJP is the result of a successful political experiment ran by members of Jan Sangh, in re-igniting the Hindu fervor through indication that the interests of the majority was being hampered due to appeasement of a handful few. However this claim of appeasement entirely falls flat when one sees the per capita income of the minorities compared to other communities or views the % share in the country's GDP. A committee report submitted post a serious study of a minority community showed how they have fallen back far behind many of the other communities in India and appeasements, if any, has definitely not helped. The political experiment also led to communal tensions in the past though the party did go strength to strength and it had its first full term government under the leadership of Atal Bihari Vajpayee from 1999 to 2004. The current PM nominee from the party has made it a habit to let out the most vituperative of speeches bringing the politics in the country to a new low. His claim of bringing an accelerated growth in Gujarat is as false as any there could be. The state has grown faster than China under the last 5 Chief Ministers. Also, 2002 riots would definitely not die from people's memory anytime soon and not to forget that NDA government under Vajpayee lost their elections 2004 despite a decent performance and against all prediction with 2002 riots playing a definite role. Also BJP has many arms and legs that though not directly linked with the party, carry out an agenda that is very regressive in its thought process and dangerous for the social fabric of the country. How could I vote for such a party who are so obsessed with one person?

Despite the above factors, I was fairly certain that I am not pressing the NOTA and definitely wanted to make my vote count. Faced with the dilemma I list out above, I went through the process of elimination. I eliminated INC and will keep them eliminated till they lose the Gandhi family, soon. I eliminated AAP thinking can't entrust the responsibility of running the country in the hand of novices who aren't still sure what they stand for. The left the BJP, but given the apprehension I had with this party and that Modi was no Vajpayee, I had to convince myself. True Modi has told many lies in his campaign, yet that he ensured the economy in Gujarat continues to do well under him was commendable, apart from industries his work in improving output in Agriculture in Gujarat through irrigation schemes and regular supply of electricity was commendable. Some of the questions that he asked during campaigns were very pertinent, including the Article 370 question in Kashmir. Also, when we could work with a remote control government, like what the UPA2 turned out to be, how bad could he get? I also had a belief that the changing scenario in the country and the push for growth would put its own pressure on political parties to modify their agenda and get rid of any archaic and regressive ideas as that would make them irrelevant. So, fear would not dictate me in keeping someone away from getting a chance. Also I am sure if they don't deliver and do falter, then in another 5 years, with more matured and politically aware electorate they would be defeated by someone who understands the needs of the times better. All in all competition is good, and this augurs well for Indian democracy. **I voted for BJP!**

# A Crash Course – MH370

Its been 9 days since the flight vanished and still all the brains of the world put together have not been able to figure out what could have happened to this flight. It is one of the biggest challenges human mind has faced in my living memory. I explore here few possible angles and the plausibility of it.

- MH370 vanished on 8th March 2014
- Before it vanished it was supposedly flying at a height of 45000ft above sea level

**The Crash Theory:**

- There are two ways of detecting a flight
  - o **Primary radar** which works on signals that bounce off the body of the plane
  - o **Secondary radar** which is dependent on response from the flight's transponder
- The crew could have switched off the on-board transponder or it could have malfunctioned
- No – reasons why the primary radar would not have detected the MH370 even if the pilot lost control and it scuttled to a crash
- If the flight was indeed in danger then the pilot should have been able to send out a distress signal

- If every system on-board malfunctioned and the flight did crash into the sea then the debris should not have been this difficult to find

## The Explosion Theory

- Something catastrophic that could prevent a pilot from even sending out a distress signal is possible only and only if
  o A situation like that of Columbia space shuttle was created where the shuttle disintegrated even before the crew could react
  o Only a nuclear explosions are known to create such amount of heat that could vaporize people even before their minds could react and also blow the flight into such small undetectable pieces
  o **Nuclear scientists are exploring this angle and seeing if any radiation could be detected indicating an explosion at 45000ft above sea level**

## The Hijacking Theory

- If hijackers were indeed behind such a nuclear explosion then why would they like to die faceless and voiceless and purposeless without announcing which group they belonged to?
- If the plane did not vaproise due to nuclear explosion and was hijacked by terrorist who were smart enough to avoid the radar systems and take it to a safer location then why haven't any group staked claim to the hijack or come out with demands?

- After all what would be the purpose of hijacking a flight full of innocent passengers if not as a bargaining chip?

## A Possible Theory

- There is a much denied experiment of the famous USS Elridge conducted in 1943 which was supposedly part of a famous/infamous Quantum Teleportation experiment based on Einstein's Unified Field Theory.
- €This experiment was supposedly altered at the request of the Navy, with the new objective being solely to render the Eldridge invisible to radar. None of these allegations has been independently substantiated.
- The experiment was called Philadelphia Experiment
- Does it make sense to see if there were any **physicist on-board** who were on a paid leave from their respective universities to conduct such an experiment?

I feel that only two explanations sound logical, one is that there was an explosion which was sudden, fast and so severe that it blew everything apart in few seconds and reduced the debris into undetectable dust which is really sad and heart wrenching to think or imagine about and I hope it isn't the case from the bottom of my heart OR MH370 was chosen for an experiment that was a top secret experiment the results of which have been unpredictable and something that could be equally devastating as a crash!

# The Gangunruly Case

Sexual misconduct of any nature against women or any individual for that matter is a heinous and a highly condemnable act. Especially sexual misconduct by people in position of power and influence is even more condemnable though unfortunately such incidents are on the rise. Sports-persons of repute, high ranking politicians, high ranking public officials and people from many other walks of life have been found guilty of such acts.

In recent times India has noticed two such high profile cases almost in succession. First was that of Tarun Tejpal the editor in chief of Tehelka and Justice AK Ganguly the former judge of the Supreme Court of India. My interest gets drawn particularly towards Justice Ganguly's case due to many interesting facts that I managed to discover amidst the media frenzy and the deafening cry to have his head. I am neither a lawyer nor do I have a legal opinion about the matter. All I wanted to do was present some facts without having to conclude or take any side.

**Aug 2010** – Subramanian Swamy files **PIL against telecom licenses** in Supreme Court – Prashant Bhushan also files a PIL

**Characters Involved:**

- €Supreme Court Bench: Justice GS Singhvi and Justice **AK Ganguly**
- Accused: A Raja, K, Kanimozhi etc.
- Who represented whom?
- Ram Jethmalani argued for Kanimozhi
- **Harish Salve** argued for Telecom Operators
- Government of India: Additional Solicitor General **Indira Jaisingh**

**Feb 2012**: Bench of Justice GS Singhvi and Justice **AK Ganguly cancels 122 telecom licenses** and asks for a fresh auction.

**Feb 2012**: Justice **AK Ganguly** retires

**Dec 2012**: The supposed law intern sexual assault takes place

**May 2013**: ASG **Indira Jaisingh** on behalf of GOI files a request to review the Feb 2012 ruling by SC

**Nov 2013:** Tehelka Editor in Chief Tarun Tejpal gets arrested after information about sexual misconduct leaks out to the media

**Nov 2013**: Law Intern blogs and indicates sexual misconduct of AK Ganguly

**Dec 2013:** Government of India (Congress/UPA) moves Presidential Reference against AK Ganguly

**Jan 2014**: AK Ganguly resigns from the post of WBHRC

I would end this blog with few statements made by various people in relation to this matter:

**Soli Sorabjee**: if Justice Ganguly resigned on merely allegations made against him and when he found no merit in them, it would set a "dangerous precedent".

**Somnath Chatterjee** The manner in which Ganguly had to step down was not only unfair and objectionable but also unconstitutional. He was denied a fair trial and the entire episode smacks of a pre-planned conspiracy. This was done at the behest of some powerful quarters. It is a wrong precedent in our country's legal system

**Subramanian Swamy**: Anyone can make allegations. Why should Justice Ganguly resign? There is no FIR. The law intern has only made allegations. Justice Ganguly shouldn't resign on the basis of allegations

**Indira Jaising**: When a person is holding a position of trust then even on slightest suspicion of misconduct which may amount to crime later, the person concerned should resign immediately

**Harish Salve:** Our judges are supposed to be worthy of being worshipped. The interns who work under Supreme Court judges consider them as hallowed beings. Now for a person to function in such a situation (when he is an accused) does not do well for himself or to the institution. If he wants he can go on leave. The institutional integrity should be preserved and the WBHRC head must step aside,

# Master of Art

The whole country and primarily the media have gone berserk and overboard in their attempt to give a befitting farewell to one of the most illustrious sporting personality of cricketing world. The festive season this year got prolonged due to one person's swan-song. This all definitely appears excessive, obsessive and arrogant.

There was a time in cricket when winning matches outside one's home condition became the primary sign of success and dominance. The year was 1991 and India was just opening out its door to the world and liberalization was being ushered in. It was still struggling to find its foothold in the world. Unsure, uncertain it was taking baby steps towards larger objective and it looking for an inspiration on this unknown journey. Almost in parallel was an individual, similarly unsure, uncertain and taking baby steps towards a possible incredible career. That year Indian cricket team toured Australia. It was almost taken for granted that India would be wiped out, the question was how bad? Offering resistance to the much vaunted Australian attack was no mean task. One man managed to restore respect for the entire cricket team and became source of inspiration for an entire nation and all this at the tender age of 18. He went on to score two test hundreds on that trip. Two things happened after that; the Indian economy soared and so did this young man's career.

The nation needed a hero, somebody who they could identify with someone who was their own and, it found it in a diminutive young man. He personified in many ways what we collectively were, shy, reserved, talented and eager to strike it big. I would like to view this great cricketer's career in 3 primary phases.

Giving the hope and encouragement that formidable quick bowling could be faced and one can make runs against hostile opponents, was definitely the first phase. This was also the time when India was being noticed and so was this individual for his performance and thus raising hopes of achieving his full potential.

Once the possibility was well established the next phase came when the attack was taken to the opposition. This was a changing phase for India, from being unsure, shy nation we were going towards prosperity and becoming a key player in the world stage. In parallel again was the little master, aggressive and prolific, attacking the best of bowlers and winning matches. Survival was no longer the motive, winning was. Nobody of my generation can ever forget the two matches played in Sharjah against Australia. One of the matches was interrupted by a sandstorm and the play had to be stopped for few minutes. Once the sandstorm stopped then came a whirlwind of amazing and devastating stroke play that the world had not seen thus far. Australian bowlers were ripped apart with disdain and the world acknowledged a legend.

The third and final phase comes when plenty of young talent came hurtling through, eager to carry the future of Indian cricket on their shoulders. This is the time when India had finally arrived and become a force to reckon with. These were those youngsters who rushed to coaching centers to become the next big name in Indian cricket, clearly inspired by the great cricketer's performance and conduct. By the time these youngsters could play for India the great man had not only become the most priced wicket, the chief bête noire but also a legend and part of folklore. Needless to say the younger lot turned out to be fearless and never overawed. Someone had demonstrated day in day out to them, that every attack is vulnerable.

There was a time when the hope of the entire nation depended only and only on one person. However, that person, silently but surely went about his task and inspired a whole new generation of sportsmen. To such an individual who has done such great service tirelessly for almost 2.5 decades, what farewell could ever be befitting?

# Throes of Cynicism

## 27 *Friday* Sep 2013

It is disheartening to see the growing cynicism within India about the political class and overall state of affairs. While undeniably every generation has to deal with its own crisis and we are midst of one, I wanted to point out that there is much to be proud of as well.

Despite not having the basics required to sustain a democracy like, a literate population, politically aware electorate, a basic standard of living, we continue to thrive as the largest democracy in the world.

Undoubtedly the democracy in India has its flaws but it is a rarity to see a developing country to sustain democracy (except the two years of Emergency) without at any stage slipping into a Martial Regime, like some of our neighboring countries.

Despite '***Deep Diversity***', a term that indicates a degree of diversity that could threaten integrity of a country, India manages to surge ahead as a united political state. It achieves this with a carefully planned:

- Special status to some states – provisioned in the constitution
- Not declaring any language as 'National' language
- Remaining neutral to Religion

Ending the Feudal system in India and ensuring peaceful integration of all the Princely states in the Indian Union. *Sardar Vallabhbhai Patel* demonstrated strong leadership in defining the length, breadth and the depth of the country in a very calculated manner. It has been seen in many banana republics that Martial regime or autocratic dictatorial regime manages to survive due to strong support from the Feudal lords who have a vested interest of ensuring continuity to their royal lifestyle and power over common people. This could have been the biggest threat to a democratic setup.

Post- Independence India realized very soon the need of a written constitution. Within 4 years (1951), the *Indian Constitution was drafted* and put into practice. Pakistan struggled in this process and even the thought of needing a constitution did not arise till as late as 1973!

India's survival is not due to it being a 'melting pot' (Like US) but due to it celebrating '*unity in diversity*'. The constitution very intelligently avoids use of the word 'Federal' but at the same time makes provision for distribution of power between the Centre and the State. The Constituent Assembly was more than aware of the danger of concentrated power and the ills associated with it yet they were wary of federalism given the 'deep diversities' of India. *Europe might have lesson or two to learn from India if they intend to sustain EU dream.*

The first elections in independent India were held in 1952 and since then continual *Electoral Reforms* have aided sustenance of democracy in the country. Starting from the tenure of *TN Seshan*, electoral process in India has become more accountable, transparent and fair. Despite its flaws and criticism, the system has managed to get rid of many evils that plagued the electoral process viz. rigging, booth capturing, silent rigging, ballot box exchange. The master stroke of introducing **Electronic Voting Machine** by **MS Gill** further aided improving the fairness of electoral process.

Unlike some of the post-colonial developing countries India did not depend only on World Bank or IMF for its economic growth. **Self Sufficiency** was the motto and many industries and institutes were built and some were setup through collaboration with countries that shared common goals. We have a vibrant Private sector popularly called as **India Inc** that is also expanding its ambitions on foreign turf.

**Non-Aligned Movement (NAM).** It was a master stroke. Despite the economic condition it was an act of courage to decide that India would remain neutral in the emerging Bi-Polar world (USA vs USSR). It assisted India to stand on its own feet and be the master of its own destiny. It is not uncommon for a developing country to succumb to external pressure and align with one camp or the other. While there is widespread criticism, in equal amount, however the strength and courage demonstrated should be admired by one and all.

*Ramachandra Guha said that India is a 'political experiment' never attempted before and probably never to be attempted again'*. It is unique in every possible way. We have problems, we have flaws, we have shortcomings and we have a long distance to go, however I strongly think that we need to understand that India is no way a banana republic. *We have strong institutions like the Supreme Court, Election Commission, and Constitution which form strong pillars of seeing us through troubled times*. I am sure that a politically aware youth would continue to struggle against odds and continue to pull surprises at people like **Winston Churchill** **who famously said 'India is a geographical term. It is no more a united nation than the equator.'**

# The Shear-Sunk Redemption

## <u>29 *Monday* Jul 2013</u>

I find this entire concept of Justice, Punishment and Societal norms very interesting and confusing. I made some attempts at trying to comprehend the entire system albeit I ended with more questions than answers. In the last of the <u>Justice Trilogy</u> – I attempted to understand the purpose of punishment. There were three primary objectives that emerged which are of –

- Retribution
- Deterrence
- Reformation

As was suggested in that article retribution, though obtained vicariously, was easiest to achieve provided there is a speedy disposal of a sub judice case. It is in the objective of deterrence and reformation that punishment has had limited to no impact. I think the primary reason for this is that, the society that we live in, there is little to no incentive to behave the right way and one is not a criminal unless one is caught! Beyond a point even fear of God fails to act as a deterrent.

In the society that we live in where power and money are worshiped there is no incentive for one to behave correct. Also we cannot and should not aim for a 1:1 Civil to Police ratio, hence every crime committed will neither be reported nor be punished.

Without any hard statistics at hand I would like to think that off all the people who commit crimes of any nature (traffic rule violation, drunken driving, financial, burglary, corruption, sexual harassment, tax evasion etc.) only a small percentage are reported against. Even among the ones that are reported against, lengthy legal procedure doesn't ensure punishment. Also off those that are reported against, I think, only a minuscule are declared as convict. Under such circumstances there is an immense incentive to do the wrong thing. Another big factor is that the person who earns power and money by questionable means doesn't ever suffer any form of social exclusion unless convicted; rather he is always worshiped as an intelligent man and as somebody who has figured out to manipulate the system to ones benefit. Plenty aspire to be this person hence there is no question of social exclusion at all. *I would like to believe that any amount of strict laws or stronger punishments would never be sufficient to curb or deter crime*

Under such circumstances a person who wants to do the right thing becomes the victim. Sometimes the victimization could be extreme and lead to social exclusion or ridicule as well. *I would like to propose that to curb crime and reduce corruption, public policy makers must find ways and methods to incentivize and inspire the right behavior.* It is here that the existing policies have failed. I would also like to suggest that the responsibility to inspire the right behavior is not only of the public policy makers but of all of us as well. *I don't think any major change in civic sense to corrupt practices would be seen unless collectively we all incentivize and inspire the right behavior.* There are plenty of opportunities that arise in day to day situations; it is only about recognizing them and not letting the moment pass.

If we notice how the corporate world functions, it is to a large extent dependent upon this incentive scheme.

Wrong doers are not always punished but the right doers are definitely rewarded so that more and more people aspire to do the right thing and be benefited in all possible ways. *Let me also indicate that incentives don't essentially have to be monetary in nature.* Just to give a simple example – we detest corrupt policemen or cringe at a traffic constable not managing the traffic well – but how many times have we given a complement for someone who was doing the right thing or even given a simple nod of appreciation? Under the lack of any public appreciation – what incentive does a policeman have to remain on the right path? While it may not apply to all situations – it is still worth a try and more thought.

# A Rolling Rupee gathers no Moss

## 14 *Sunday* Jul 2013

By now even school going kids know that the Rupee is falling. Since it started its southward trip in 2009, there has been no end to its fascination with it. Sometime it looks like a skydiver on a rapid decline but with the hope that the parachute would open successfully and the fall would be halted and eased till reaching a stable surface. Only that in this instance the parachute is nowhere to be seen or has malfunctioned thus continuing the rapid fall.

While it is being discussed fervently by one and all in the financial sector, many might not know how it influences all of our lives. Also it would be interesting to note if anything could be done to mitigate the situation. Here I present my analysis of the situation and possible steps to rectify the situation.

**Reasons for the fall:**

**Firstly**, we have to understand that, the Rupee is performing badly against the $ but not essentially against all currencies. So why bother at all? Unfortunately there is plenty to bother about because entire International Trade is done in and measured against the Dollar. Many transactions happen in nothing but the dollar. So, not only the Rupee but every currency in the world has to keep a track of how it measures against the dollar. On an earlier occasion I had presented an analysis to show how this benefitsAmerica.

**Secondly**, this situation can be viewed as a simple case of demand and supply. There is demand for $ but shortage of supply. We know from our common sense that this would undoubtedly lead to increase of the cost of that commodity. That's exactly what happened. We have to spend more Rupees to buy the same amount of $, in other words $ has indeed become expensive!

**Thirdly**, why is $ in short supply and why is there a demand for it? Unfortunately to buy Petrol and Gold any some of the other imports we have to spend $. Which means people have to use their Rupees to buy $ and then use the $ to buy the imports. So the $ quantity in country reduces. So we can see why there is a demand. There is an uptake in demand for the yellow metal and hence more $ than usual is used up to buy Gold hence creating a shortage.

**Fourthly**, we are also unable to increase the supply of $. Why? Because we don't control the printing of $ and there is a decrease in interest to invest in India. So FII and FDI have pulled funds out of the country. Also announcement by Fed that it is looking at ending the quantitative easing (more $) as its economy seems to be well on the path of recovery has meant that there is a sudden rush in the market to buy $ now. These $ would be part of forex reserves and when the $ actually reduces in the market the $ reserves would rise in value and help in buying goods for cheap. So both these points put together there is a shortage of $.

**Fifthly**, India's current deficit is increasing. Which means we import more than we export or we receive less of $ compared to the $ we send out. Even though with the falling Rupee Indian Exports become cheaper –but the macroeconomic situation in Europe and America is contributing to lesser consumption of exportable goods.

## Impact of a Falling rupee

### Beneficial for Some:

For all the organization who are dependent on export, this is a great time to earn revenue as every $ they earn gives them more Rupees.

The family of those people who work abroad and remit their earnings periodically.

### Detrimental for Some:

Any organization that is dependent on importing material for its own productivity would find these imports more expensive and hence an impact to their overall health.

### Overall impact:

Government of India which relies heavily on imports of essential fossil fuels or other items would find a heavy drag on its exchequer, as all the imports become expensive.

Increased expenditure of the Government will mean lower revenues which could be made up only by increasing cost of products or tax on products

Inflation would increase and impact the common man

With already more Rupee chasing less $, RBI cannot cut any key rates thus leading to stifling of economic activity.

**What could possibly be done to stem the fall of the rupee? Here Government policies and RBI intervention are critical to recovering the situation.**

- Increase $ in the market
- RBI needs to sell its reserves to increase the $ availability in the market (already done)
- Making Remittance more attractive – more $ inflow into the country
- Discourage import of Gold (attempted by RBI by imposing fresher tax)
- Decrease dependency on imports
- Increase FDI and hence increase inflow of $ (no wonder Chidambaram is in the USA)
- Join China in the demand for a neutral currency like IMF SDR for international trade

# Squares-Root of Revolution

When we think squares – we think a perfectly symmetric geometric shape. The name which invokes a symmetric imagery has been at the center of many disruptive developments across the world. Removed from the theoretical geometric space and brought into practical urban public spaces, these squares all of a sudden became household names and ushered in unthinkable revolution. I know human beings react differently to different type of spaces and pseudo-scientific fields like Feng Shui or Vaastu Shashtra might also have some inputs regarding shapes and energy levels. All said and then Squares have become epitome of humanitarian struggle against indifferent authority. **Squares in urban spaces was an European concept that have been improvised and adapted by other schools of city planners and architects. Many improvised and adapted versions of public squares have had presences in many countries outside of Europe.**

In the modern times, lot has changed due to continual human struggle against disturbing but established and accepted notions/norms. We witnessed people, questioning a form of economic development championed by capitalist, protesting against age old form of governance, challenging people in power to formulate rules for benefit of larger section of population, upholding the morality of a State in execution of its duty; and many more. Again, at the center of most of these protests are Squares. Squares that today have become synonymous with human struggle for a dignified living.

The squares that have become popular for the platform it gave for people to speak and be heard and hold anybody in authority accountable are:

- **Tiananmen Square – Beijing China – Student uprising 1979**
- **Shahyad Square – Tehran, Iran – Anti-Election protests 2010-11**
- **Times Square – New York, USA – Occupy Wall Street 2011**
- **Tahrir Square – Cairo, Egypt – Arab Spring 2011-12**
- **Al-Tahrir Square – Sana'a Yemen – Arab Spring 2011-12**
- **Shahbag Square – Dhaka, Bangladesh – Protest for justice against war crimes 2013**

These are the ones that one can recall without much effort, am sure there are more. Place de la Concorde or the French Revolution square comes to my mind. A square at the center of as significant a historical event as the French revolution in the 18th century.

Ofcourse, only history can be the true judge of success or failure of such protests/revolution, We live in times where there are inequities and many other social evils that question the very core of human beliefs. However, we should take heart in the fact that, whenever people have come together and voiced their concern unanimously – those voices, through conviction and constancy of purpose have brought unprecedented change. **Squares could be mere co-incidence!**

# Speaking Free

## <u>14 *Thursday* Feb 2013</u>

Freedom of speech/expression is the mantra of our times. Everywhere and anywhere somebody is either using it or violating it or abusing it or getting upset by it. People are debating about it, fighting over it and even getting arrested for it. Suddenly it is being held aloft as the most coveted possession of a democratic state and as something to be safeguarded at all costs. Some, who exercise it, take a moral high ground and feel offended if they are stopped from exercising it or are blamed for excesses. News channels, often blamed for excess, are the new self-proclaimed champions of 'Freedom of speech'; most appear to know the constitution inside out and take a moral high ground on related matters. Also thanks to social networking sites, many more unlikely champions have emerged and gain some following as well.

What is freedom of speech? Is it really a hallmark of democracy as it is made out to be? Are my rights violated when I am not allowed to express? What if somebody gets emotionally hurt or insulted because of my right of freedom of speech?

Let us look back at our day to day lives. Do we really ever feel at any stage that we cannot express what we want to express? Whether it is our coffee shop/tea stall casual chat or living room casual discussion or dinner table discussion – do we really feel that for some reason we are not free to express what we want to say? I am sure I don't have to answer these rhetoric questions. I have been to China and have many Chinese friends; did I in any interaction feel they were not free to express what they wanted to say? No! On the contrary they were quite expressive. Expressive to the extent of telling me their view points about the Cultural Revolution and the student uprising at Tiananmen Square, not a hint of stifled freedom of speech. So our fundamental right as a human being without having to follow a constitutional diktat seems to be intact. Ofcourse nobody can deny that, there is certain amount of self-policing, at times voluntarily, to avoid hurting sentiments of people who we are expressing our views to. Nonetheless, we all, no matter where we are born, are free to speak! So the question repeats again – what is freedom of speech that we are breaking our head over?

Now imagine if any of the opinions expressed by us in a private conversation was to find its way to a publicly accessible forum/medium! Suddenly do we feel our heart stop or we stopping in our stride? I think herein could lie the true definition of Freedom of Speech. Are all the opinions expressed in private conversation ok to be expressed in a publicly accessible forum? Would we express everything in public what we say in private? In expressing our opinion in public we always run the risk of saying something that is unacceptable to some. These are the things that test the tolerance level and also expose hypocrisy of a society. Thus I feel that, Freedom of speech exists in all countries irrespective of the form of governance it has; the main issue is of tolerance and double standards.

What one feels is what one should say. If done in a private conversation nobody bothers. If done in a public forum then the said word has repercussions. Tolerance level of the society decides the threshold; beyond that point it could be considered as deliberate attempt to spread vile and hatred. However not saying what I feel about things and instead to say what would be widely accepted on a public forum exposes the double standard and hypocrisy in a society. It is a fight between Tolerance level and Double Standards. In case of a non-democratic Government Tolerance levels are very low and double standards extremely high. In the case of a perfect democracy Tolerance levels are very high and double standards very low. Most of the countries are, obviously, between these two extremes.

Social networking sites present a new type of dilemma. They are private yet they are public, they are public yet they are private. These sites are neither in the mold of a traditional public forum nor are they equivalent to roadside tea stalls/coffee shops. Expressed opinions here are private, yet are public. With plenty of government organization/officials joining such sites in official capacity, makes the medium that much more interesting. Opinions expressed on such sites with the type of following they command can, theoretically, lead to instantaneous repercussions and at times to immediate backlash on the expresser of the opinion. Everybody ofcourse is free to express their opinion, however the medium is so unprecedented and the repercussions so much unstudied that there is an apprehension. The dilemmatic nature of the medium doesn't make it any easier either. So the dilemma has led to lowering of tolerance levels fortunately though, it has not led to increase in double standards. On the contrary it has brought it down by an extent.

As the medium matures and repercussions become clearer, I am sure; certain amount of self-policing would come in. As has happened in a personal one-to-one conversations. I should also mention that achieving a balance between Tolerance levels and Double Standard cannot be a matter of chance nor can it be achieved overnight. It has to be deliberate and would be a slow and steady process.

# Despised at home
# Loved Abroad

America is often referred to as the land of opportunities. Many have made use of the opportunities on offer and struck it big. There is a strong unmistakable entrepreneurial spirit that is omnipresent, especially if you are in a place like the Silicon Valley and I felt it was difficult to remain immune from it.. I had the privilege of being at the heart of Silicon Valley and see many of those organizations who from their humble beginnings in a garage or a backyard, went onto become large multinational conglomerates and household names across the world

Infact when in this country, one realizes that there are many more large corporations, probably just as bigger as the American firms we know, and yet they never left the shores of USA to explore business opportunities elsewhere. Exemplary customer service and good products have ensured a strong business in the US. Nothing in the Silicon Valley even remotely hints of any recession. Restaurants are running full, retail outlets are bustling with customers, and roads are busy with traffic.

Amidst all these observation, the most interesting and surprising observation I had was that of a paradox! A paradox, that appears to exist in the general American psyche. A paradox that is as funnier as it is surprising! Let me explain. As we know there are many hugely successful US enterprises who have not only done exceptionally well in America but also in many of the countries where they also setup their operations in. Among them, not all but, few handful of organizations are reserved for 'awe', 'love' 'affection' and 'Pride' in the American Psyche. Many American organizations have to face tremendous and widespread public hatred at home and here in lays the paradox. These hated orgs, make no mistake, are huge and successful across the world. The paradox becomes even more interesting when many of the orgs that are hated here are loved overseas and seen synonymous with the American Culture.

It is a syndrome of "Despised at home, loved elsewhere" Any American worth his or her salt wouldn't like to be seen doing anything with these despised organizations! A middle class American wouldn't like to be seen shopping in Wal-Mart, eating in McDonalds or Pizza Hut and driving Dodge. Even if an American is doing all of the above he wouldn't like to be caught doing it! The case of Wal-Mart is worth a special mention here. Not only is it widely hated but I felt it also shows the class-divide in an American society. There are three classes, as per me, a Class that shops in Wal-Mart by choice, a class that shops at Wal-Mart by compulsion and a class that stays away from Wal-Mart under all circumstances. Infact the ones shopping by choice make all attempts to show they are doing it out of compulsion, the ones who are doing out of compulsion wouldn't like to be caught in the act! Known for poor business ethics, poor work atmosphere, low pay and plethora of cheap Chinese made goods, I haven't seen or heard any other org singled out for such choicest abuses, widespread hatred and yet be No1 (No.2) Fortune 500 company! Therein lays the Paradox!

There are many more such examples. Ofcourse not all large organizations are hated, though their record might be no different than Wal-Mart. There are few that are nonetheless reserved for widespread Awe, love, affection and what every American would like to identify with or take pride in. Apple, Starbucks, Cosco are some names that I could immediately remember based on the interactions I had. There are status symbols everywhere and America is no different, however the paradoxical nature of these symbols is what made it very interesting to observe.

# El camino a la prosperidad

## 28 *Monday* Jan 2013

Excellent Customer Service, that's what is screaming out loud from every store, every restaurant, every nook and corner. Right from the time when one enters a place to the time when one leaves it's all about customer service and customer delight.

Walk in to a store or a restaurant and there is somebody with you in few seconds, greeting you with a smile and asking if they could be of any help. Promptly letting you know the options and choices at offer and making every effort to understand your needs. Yes, most of it is process driven so that, every customer gets a consistent level of service, yet there is plenty of customer delight brought in by going the extra mile. For example, greeting when, you step in, to ensuring you get what you want, to wishing you a great day before you leave is great customer service, however throwing in freebies or customizing an item or offering additional options of value is customer delight!

Great customer service is always about, clear and prompt communication, appropriate response to customer's reaction, unintimidating method of guidance and honesty. Anything over and above this leads to customer delight. I have seen so many instances of that. This country is about entrepreneurship – huge retail outlets, restaurant chains, fast food chains, family owned businesses, large corporations including banks, some are now MNCs and some never left the shores of this country. Yet what combines them in uniqueness of character is – customer service.

They say that customer service can be only as good as your products, however the humility, respect and dedication towards service is very endearing and I think a thing to be learnt and adapted wherever possible. It is business success through human touch.

# Brandishing

## 08 *Tuesday* Jan 2013

Country of origin or Country of birth is often a very emotional and personal affair. We believe our dedication to our country of birth or origin is beyond reason and to be absolute. Patriotism has always been a matter of passion and emotion and treated ahead of logic and reasoning. What if we were to change this status quo and just as a hypothesis look at this equation of Nation/State – Citizen, relationship from the view point of a Product and Consumer viewpoint? A sudden chain of thought that got triggered while attending a short course on marketing and branding.

What struck me was, what if we start treating a country and it's policies as a product and the citizen as the consumer of this Product? What if, like in the case of any other Product, brand loyalty is driven not by compulsion but by choice! A brand is supposed to have an USP and should build its brand equity on the basis of the value proposition it offers to the consumer. The experience that a consumer gets by choosing a product drives his loyalty towards a particular brand. Now let us replace brand with country/state and its policy, also we will replace consumer with citizen. A country needs to drive patriotism by voluntary choice of the citizen or atleast, it should appear so. A country should make it clear as to what it 'stands for' and what its values are, and what it has to offer with respect to quality of life and opportunities of growth. These, form the core of its USP. A country has the responsibility of making it clear to its citizens what benefits it has to offer if they were to choose to be its citizen and how it would be a value addition to their respective lives. The quality of life one gets in a country and experiences one has should drive a person's loyalty towards a country. What I would not explore here is the concept of competing brands and a consumer (citizen) having the choice to switch brands depending upon desired quality of life and the value-proposition. (does happen now).

This could appear to be a blasphemous thought to many and ofcourse what I present is only a hypothesis. Though selling country as a brand is not a new idea. Countries have been doing this for ages to attract tourists or top brains and talent from across the world, however selling it as a brand to its own citizen might be a proposition that hasn't been explored much. On a serious note, by building brand equity for itself, a country could help improve unity among people, boost morale, boost self-image and this could have positive effect on the economy. I thought this was a radical idea, however a quick search on the internet proved me wrong. The concept of Nation-Branding for domestic consumption has been doing the rounds for the past decade or so and the Government in conjunction with the elite have been entrusted with the onus of building the brand equity to drive loyalty of its citizen.

# Rape And Society

The news that has made and been making headlines across the world, including China, is the incident of brutal rape of a 23 year old paramedic student in Delhi. The details of the incident are ghastly and stomach churning and yet the brave lady had this to say to her Mom "I want to live", an exemplary demonstration of courage and fighting spirit that at times only women can demonstrate. It is unfortunate that as I write this post in the New Year, the lady is no more and I have no hesitation is saying that she died a martyr's death. A Martyr dies for a cause and I think today the whole world has acknowledged the cause that this lady died for. Ofcourse she has expanded the canvas and has made attempts to ask questions much beyond just this brutal incident. I salute the lady's spirit, spare a moment of silence to mourn her death and offer heartfelt condolences to the bereaved family. We all are answerable and responsible for what happened to her.

**Myths about Rape and Sexual Violence:**

Her martyrdom doesn't seem to have gone waste as people on social media, roadside stalls, schools, colleges and offices across the world have reacted, expressed anguish and debated preventive measures along with apt punishments for perpetrators of such crimes. It has also raised plenty of questions about safety of women in society and an even larger question of how much freedom does a society give to its women. It has also led to a parochial view point about the Indian society at large being misogynist and being outpaced by the rapid westernization or modernization of people. I think before we jump to conclusions and find out why such crimes are committed, few facts need to be sorted out dispassionately, and then we could embark on a journey to remedy the Indian Society.

- Rape or Sexual violence against women is an universal phenomenon
- Developed Economies have significant cases of sexual violence against women as Developing economies
- Sex ratio of a country has nothing to do with increase or decrease in incidents of rape
- Conviction rates in all countries continues to be low if not lower than India
- All incidents of such nature do not get reported to the police in other countries as well
- All countries have their own degree of issues with respect to Women's liberty or freedom
- Research done on Chemical Castration shows it is not proven to be effective always
- Rape is not a modern society problem
- Rape is as much common in rural areas as it is in urban areas so women's dress definitely is not an instigator
- The marital status or age of the criminal is not a factor, married or old men too rape

**Role of Literature and Media:**

Literature in all languages and forms (prose or poetry) has always glorified the female body and it continues unabated.

From the print media it has now moved to an audio visual format and ofcourse has titillated the male senses for some quite some time. So the objectification of women is complete. A society which struggles to give freedom to women or has issues in providing equal opportunities to women or has repressed sexual behavior, combined with objectification of women, has often led to the male dismissing any right of dignity and respect to the women folk. The problems has gotten more complicated with lot of women, impressed by the audio visual representation, have started to see themselves as "sexy" or objects of "sexual desire". However a society that believes in respect and dignity to a women and level playing ground wouldn't dare to see anyone violate the personal space of a lady. Every incident of sexual violence against women is invariably a violation of the dignity, respect and personal choice that a woman deserves and demands of a society. I would repeat here that this is not an Indian problem per say, it is a universal problem; however the degree of the problem definitely varies depending upon the dynamics of respective societies.

**Protesters and the Mindset:**

I often find it interesting to note protests in situation where we are in a way protesting against ourselves. A rapist, as I mentioned in a blog earlier, are not aliens. They are part of the same society and are one among us. Government can't be held responsible and should not be held responsible for anything and everything. For example female foeticide is a societal phenomenon and our parents and family members who feel burdened by a girl child or ask for dowry during marriages are to be blamed for such situations and no amount of policing can ever stop such tacit acts. Infact sometimes such acts are perpetrated by women themselves. Many among those who protest would cringe at the idea of their daughter's or sisters having the freedom to choose a career or a life partner entirely on her own or even decide on the hours allowed outside home. Societal changes are not easy to come about especially where the problem is chronic in nature. Yet that's exactly what the current problem demands. Question that one has to ask is what aides such societal changes, what aides in change of age old mindsets? What incentivizes people to move out of their comfort zone and ask questions? I think there is a strong need for social scientists or sociologists with strong relevance to India to develop innovative solutions after studying various co-related or unrelated data. I wouldn't be surprised if nobody among the protestor is inspiring their kids to be social scientists or sociologists and assist in transforming society through innovative methods. Unless people start doing things that they haven't done before, they won't get results that haven't been seen before.

**Part of a Solution or Part of a Problem:**

Debate has raged on how to appropriately punish the criminals who commit such crimes. The question ofcourse goes beyond just sexual violence and expands to what true justice is. Capital punishment that is being demanded would in a way end the criminal's agony in one shot whereas the victim or their family would have to suffer all their life, yet if life imprisonment is awarded then the prisoner survives all his life on tax payers money and yet some would say that an opportunity for the person to repent, reform and become productive and reenter society is what we should aim for. And the debate continues with no perfect answer to the problem, especially in the case of rape or any incident of sexual violence.

I think there are three key aspects to think about in the Indian context

- Reduce female foeticide/ infanticide
- Prevention of Sexual violence
- Strict laws that are appropriately implemented to deal with any incidents of sexual violence
- Rehabilitation of the victim

Let us explore some possible solutions that I could think of, and I don't indicate this to be a exhaustive list by any stretch of imagination or arrogance.

## Reduce female foeticide/ infanticide:

- Incentivize families with girl child – addition quote under PDS or free education till a particular age
- Incentivize states with better sex ratio with greater fund allocation
- Incentivize colleges or schools with greater girl representation

## Prevention of Sexual violence:

- Street lights have a strong co-relation with crimes in general and sexual violence in specific
- Provide Police patrolling in crime prone areas 24x7x365
- Caste system needs to be dealt with as upper caste men have been known to demonstrate superiority by raping women of lower caste

- Families and Parents have to teach to their sons about the equal rights that women have in this world and that they need to be protected
- Increase the reporting of events so that more and more people get exposed [Needs police to have a mindset of not blaming the victim]- so people get discouraged to perform such crimes in the future
- Increase the conviction rates – so reporting increases and it also in turn acts as a deterrent
- Increasing conviction rates and reporting of such incidents needs a proper redressal system which I describe below

**Strict laws that are appropriately implemented to deal with any incidents of sexual violence and Rehabilitation of the victim:**

- In countries like Denmark, Canada and US there is a special Task force created to deal with Rape victims
- This task force is responsible for providing a multi-disciplinary (paramedics, doctors, psychotherapist, lawyers) approach to dealing with the victim's issues
- The task force is responsible for collecting evidences for forensic activities
- Only and only if the victim agrees for the information to be exposed or reported do the police get involved
- If a victim directly goes to the Police the police after filing a report transfer the victim to the task force
- These task forces have branches in major hospitals across country
- More Fast Track courts that function every day to expedite delivery of justice

No changes happen overnight, no changes happen without. All changes take time, are painful and also have to start from within. Ofcourse we need to start somewhere, the earlier we start the earlier we reach milestones, though the journey never ends.

# About Guns and Women

## 22 *Saturday* Dec 2012

Two incidents in America and India respectively have led to widespread heated discussion. The incidents I refer to are shootout in a school in the US and Gang rape in India. While both incidents are obviously isolated, yet the discussion that has ensued in respective countries has had overlapping repercussions. America questions the freedom to own firearms and probably use the incident in India to justify lesser Gun Control and on the other hand India questions should we have greater freedom of owning firearms so that incident like what we witnessed doesn't happen. Two seemingly different incidents have common factors; both are a reflection of the Politics and Society of the respective countries and both the incidents were equally gruesome, brutal and leave us horrified, shocked and with many answerless questions.

**America Debates:**

The firearm makers' association has long lobbied in favor of allowing greater freedom in firearm ownership. The rationale behind such a step was that a country is not free, just and democratic unless ordinary people get to choose if they intend to own firearms or not. A society cannot be just if only criminals possess firearms, albeit illegally, commit crimes with them and yet ordinary citizens can't legally possess firearms which could help them protect themselves. The legislation was welcomed and people felt that knowing that ordinary citizen possess weapons, crime rates should come down. The argument definitely sounds logical, favorable and convincing. However what was not factored in was the chance of these firearms occasionally landing in the hands of depressed, manic and deranged individuals who were capable of doing unthinkable shocking acts. The current incident was not the first time that we had a certain individual opening fire in a public place that lead towards loss of lives of children and adults alike, however the loss of lives of 20 children and 6 adults leaves plenty of questions to be answered. Some would argue that America needs newer rules of gun control and yet some would argue that if the school teacher possessed a firearm hidden somewhere in her drawer, lot of lives could have been saved.

For all the lobbying that happens, for all the firearms that get sold and for all the occasional shootouts that happen in public places what would be of interest to see is, if ownership of firearms had a strong co-relation with crime rates? Let me provide some comparative data

| Indicator | Country/Territory | ISO code | Source | % of homicides by firearm | Number of homicides by firearm | Homicide by firearm rate per 100,000 pop | Rank by rate of ownership | Average firearms per 100 people | Average total all civilian firearms |
|---|---|---|---|---|---|---|---|---|---|
| Countries with lower rate of Firearm ownership | West Bank & Gaza | PS | CTS | 72.4 | 105 | 2.95 | 118 | 3.4 | 125000 |
| | Egypt | EG | CTS | 69.1 | 453 | 0.57 | 115 | 3.5 | 1900000 |
| | Azerbaijan | AZ | CTS | 6.5 | 11 | 0.12 | 115 | 3.5 | 290000 |
| | Turkmenistan | TM | CTS | 2.4 | 6 | 0.1 | 114 | 3.8 | 180000 |
| | Netherlands | NL | NSO | 30.7 | 56 | 0.33 | 112 | 3.9 | 510000 |
| | India | IN | CTS | 7.6 | 3093 | 0.26 | 110 | 4.2 | 46000000 |
| | Cambodia | KH | NGO | 36.7 | 187 | 1.44 | 109 | 4.3 | 600000 |
| | Zimbabwe | ZW | CTS | 65.6 | 598 | 4.76 | 106 | 4.4 | 400000 |
| | Taiwan | TW | Ministry of Justice | 16.9 | 126 | 0.56 | 106 | 4.4 | 725000 |
| | Philippines | PH | WHO-MDB | 49.9 | 7349 | 8.93 | 105 | 4.7 | 3900000 |
| | Cuba | CU | WHO-MDB | 4.4 | 27 | 0.24 | 104 | 4.8 | 545000 |
| | Dominican Republic | DO | SES/National police | 65.5 | 1618 | 16.3 | 99 | 5.1 | 450000 |
| | Bahamas | BS | CTS | 61.2 | 62 | 15.37 | 98 | 5.3 | 17000 |
| Countries with higher rate of Firearm ownership | United States | US | CTS | 60 | 9146 | 2.97 | 1 | 88.8 | 2.7E+08 |
| | Switzerland | CH | CTS | 72.2 | 57 | 0.77 | 3 | 45.7 | 3400000 |
| | Finland | FI | CTS | 19.8 | 24 | 0.45 | 4 | 45.3 | 2400000 |
| | Serbia | RS | CTS | 33.1 | 45 | 0.46 | 5 | 37.8 | 3050000 |
| | Cyprus | CY | CTS | 26.3 | 5 | 0.46 | 6 | 36.4 | 275000 |
| | Uruguay | UY | CTS | 46.5 | 93 | 2.8 | 8 | 31.8 | 1100000 |
| | Sweden | SE | CTS | 33.9 | 37 | 0.41 | 10 | 31.6 | 2800000 |
| | Norway | NO | WHO-HFA | 8.1 | 2 | 0.05 | 11 | 31.3 | 1400000 |
| | France | FR | WHO-MDB | 9.6 | 35 | 0.06 | 12 | 31.2 | 19000000 |
| | Canada | CA | CTS | 32 | 173 | 0.51 | 13 | 30.8 | 9950000 |
| | Austria | AT | CTS | 29.5 | 18 | 0.22 | 14 | 30.4 | 2500000 |
| | Germany | DE | CTS/National police | 26.3 | 158 | 0.19 | 15 | 30.3 | 25000000 |

As the data would show, the % of homicides due to firearms in countries with lower ownership rates is not much different than the countries with higher ownership rates. Also *America is turning out to be a bad example to quote if owning of firearms has to be advocated. Homicide rate in America is the highest among the countries with high ownership.* The country that comes second with respect to ownership of firearms has an almost 50% lower ownership rate and a much lower crime rate compared to America. I think the writing is definitely on the wall and America has quite a problem on hand to deal with. I am not sure if it could afford to wait till another similar incident happens before rethinking gun control; however lobbying will not make it an easy job.

**India Debates:**

Various Women welfare organizations are fighting hard to mete out capital punishment to the perpetrators of the heinous crime of rape in the recent incident that happened in Delhi. Undoubtedly it is a heart wrenching, spine chilling and extremely gruesome crime that anybody could commit. The question being asked is a crime that leaves the victim dealing with a lifelong mental trauma, what would be the most appropriate and severe punishment that could be awarded to the criminals which is just and at same time exemplary enough to act as a deterrent in the future. Some argue that capital punishment is most appropriate, others would counter argue saying, the victim has to suffer all her life so an appropriate punishment should make the rapist suffer as much, and hence propose chemical castration as the right punishment. Yet there are many who suggest that existing laws or any amount rules would never act as a deterrent enough, instead we should have lesser gun control and have access to firearms. There could be no bigger deterrent than that ever and would lead to reduction in all forms of crime.

Talking about Gun control, the above graph presented could not link higher firearm ownership and lower crime rates in any definite manner. In addition another data shown in the graphs below for *America* again don't show any emerging co-relation either, the ***decrease in incidents of rape in America was not linked with corresponding increase in ownership of firearms!***

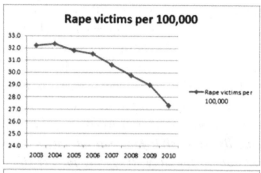

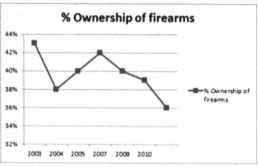

I think, the larger question that is being asked is who was responsible for such crime, police? Politicians? Society? The Victim? It is true that the Politicians don't treat rape as a key issue of discussion as it doesn't give them any votes and police often lack the sensitivity to deal with such issues. I think the problem is with our Society at large and the views of Police and Politicians are only a reflection of the society they represent. I indicated in an earlier blog post that whenever such incidents happen the society has to take collective responsibility. Yes there are widespread protests, there are demands for capital punishment, and there are talks about ostracizing the perpetrators. However for a society where women can't wear what she wants, can't get married to who she wants to, can't chose career as per her interest and a society where even birth of a girl child is at the mercy of the males, in such a society such protests appear farcical. Rape is an instance of a disrespectful male that doesn't think much about women liberty or freedom. The society that has so vociferously condemned the current crime would not blink to say that women should dress appropriately or should not stay out till late night or should have been married off in her teens. *We are all equally responsible for what has happened we are all answerable to the lady struggling for her life and to her family and to all such victims. It is unfortunate but a society gets the police, politicians and crime it deserves.*

# Routing Madness

A first Visit to any city is always associated with equal amount of excitement and anxiety. While the excitement is well understood, point to ponder about is what are we anxious about? I guess the anxiety is always about the new people we are going to meet and what their reaction would be towards us. Visitors who land in cities unknown to them have some form of 'visitors' or 'strangers' or 'outsiders' tag stuck to their foreheads. I don't know what exactly it is, twitch of the nose? Move of the eye? Unsure walk? Providers of a service, like cab drivers, are very good at figuring that out and sometimes exploit it as well. Last thing we want upon reaching a place is, to be conned. I remember a funny scene from a not so popular Bollywood movie; the scene shows a bunch of friend land in a city unknown to them, the cab driver recognizes instantly that these are "out of Towner's" and literally takes them for a 'ride'; While going round and round in circles around the city one of the friend notices seeing a particular shop again and again. When the person asks the driver that I thought I saw that shop an hour ago, the driver answers to that saying 'it's a very popular shop and has a branch in almost all localities of the city so don't be surprised if you see it again and again' quite convincing isn't it?

As humans we always look for assurances. Personally I have this need to feel a bit more in control about matters such as explained above and still keep my adventurous side alive. Today *Mobile Devices, Global Positioning System, (GPS) and Google Maps* have played a tremendous role in allaying my fears and soothing my nerves. They are making unfamiliar cities familiar. By making these cities familiar they are helping me feel connected to the place. Cities and towns open up to me and speak to me like never before. Presence of GPS and Google Maps in the city I am visiting means that I know distance from the Airport to the hotel, I can calculate approximately how much it would cost and how much time it should take and also figure out what are the interesting things on the way. It has never failed me till date and has the capability of picking up even the seemingly obscure locations/landmark. With this control back in my hand and nerves soothed, I can focus more on enjoying my journey and talk to the people around with greater assurance. It has helped me focus on people and helped me to strike up interesting of conversation with strangers and make friendships in places that I could have never imagined before.

Technology always, like many others things, is a double edged sword, used appropriately it reduces distances between humans and used in excess creates imaginary distances where none existed. Sometimes we feel more comfortable to SMS our neighbor than walk across and have chat! Nonetheless I would still inspire everyone to trust GPS/Google maps as it makes life easier when travelling. I have often surprised cab drivers or friends with the amazing level of accuracy with which I could guide them or drive them to the required destination. The irony is, that I needed satellites residing miles above the surface of the earth to help me feel comfortable in going from one place to the other on earth

# Inflated Conspiracy

Every time my cousin comes visiting to India from the US of A, he always ends of complaining how the cost of living has dramatically gone up since the last time he came to India. Each time he comes, his hopes of relocating to India keeps getting dimmer, as he looks at the ***spiraling costs and the incomparable standards of living***. This is a rather interesting point, US with such high standard of living manages to maintain a significantly low cost of living or inflation. ***Inspite of subsidy that it gives to farmers and the cheaper than cheap fuel (called gasoline) it offers, the cost of living continues to be low and the standard of living significantly high. Paradoxical!***

I present a theory, not mine, but a view point that I endorse to and that has existed for quite some time and dismissed by many as 'one of the many conspiracy theories' that does not merit any attention or time. However, a closer scrutiny might indicate that, this theory cannot be dismissed outright. Even if the effects are not deliberate but nonetheless the outcomes are unmistakable. To understand the theory, three facts need to be understood by us:

- **Most countries like to keep their Forex Reserves in the form of Dollars**
- **All currencies in the world are equated against the Dollar for it's value in the market**

- **Dollar circulation is entirely managed by an Independent central Bank – Federal Reserve (Fed) in the US of A.**

Fed decides the Monetary Policy independent of the world economic scenario. Whenever USA prints more Dollars and makes money easily available with almost 0% interest rates, the money invariably finds it's way into the international market via MNCs or FIIs and into other countries as Forex. Two situations arise due to this:

### *Situation 1*

- **More the Dollars in a country = the local currency 'appreciates'**
- **The more the local currency appreciates the more expensive it's exports become [imports become cheaper]**
- **More expensive the exports the less competitive the Country gets in International trade scene**

### *Situation 2*

- **Lesser the Dollars in a country than local currency = the local currency 'depreciates'**
- **The more the local currency depreciates the more expensive the imports become [exports become competitive]**
- **More expensive the imports the more expensive the Cost of living becomes in the domestic scene**
- **More money in circulation also causes domestic inflation**

This is the Catch 22 situation of the top order, getting the balance right is not an easy policy decision for any government. Nonetheless an export oriented Developing or Developed Economy can in no way afford to be non-competitive in the International Market, hence invariably the second of the above two options gets chosen. ***Observe how the price at which US buys products from these countries remains relatively stable helping them keep imports cheap and also by ensuring most of the printed dollars move out of the country they manage to keep a very low inflation***. However the Cost of living in the country that is exporting the goods becomes high, due to dearer imports and high amount of local currency in circulation. So in this manner, whether deliberately or unintentionally US exports its inflation by ensuring – There is steady supply of dollars and continuity of international trade in dollars.

China, the emerging super power and an export oriented developing economy, probably understood this much earlier than others and ensured that their RMB or Chinese Yuan remains rock steady in value versus the Dollar. They tried to keep the value of their currency decoupled from Dollar, so they could continually remain competitive in International Trade and at the same time control prices locally and fuel domestic growth. Ofcourse all of this came at the expense of being called a ***"Currency Manipulator"***, however their objective was met. Other countries with lesser clout than China – do suffer the consequences of Dollar supply. China also has been the most vocal in asking for the International Trade to be done in a neutral currency [***Ex: using the SDR of IMF***] so the world trade is decoupled from Dollar whose circulation is dictated by Fed entirely based on the domestic requirement in the USA.

So the message I got to give my cousin is, because Cost of Living in India is going up, because US is able to maintain steady or low cost of living and this situation is not expected to change as long as US continues it's two major exports:

- **Dollars**

**and hence**

- **Inflation**

# Nations of a State and States of a Nation

## 21 *Wednesday* Nov 2012

Life has to get precedence over all other beliefs and laws of society. Death of **Savita Halappanavar**, in Ireland is unacceptable and intolerable under any circumstances. It raises strong questions about 'Statehood' and influence of religion and again brings forth the debate of Nation vs State. Savita did not die due to medical negligence but because of a less understood and open-to-interpretation law that bans abortion due to the religious reasons. How can a matured state allow that to happen?

We often use Nation and State as synonymous terms even though both are different. A society of men is said to constitute a **Nation** when they feel conscious of their common racial or cultural or sentimental solidarity among themselves. Contrastingly a **State** is a Political entity and bound by geography and law of land. A Nation doesn't have to be restricted to a single State and a state doesn't have to be restricted to a single nation. Often States are assimilation of multiple nations and nations are spread across multiple states. States with single Nation are called **Mono-National** and States with multiple nations and are called **Poly-National**.

Some States have traditionally been of a **Poly-National character** where as some of the others acquired this character over a period of time and yet there are some that want to staunchly protect their coveted ***Mono-National character***. Rapidly changing demographics have started putting pressure on the Mono-National States and have put them in a dilemma. These States on one hand open their doors to foreign nationals and fill shortage of human resource with specific skills and at the same time try to ensure it in no way threatens their local electorate. Invariably, the foreign nationals arrive with their own cultural baggage. These baggages start weighing heavily upon the local culture and threaten continuity of culture in the existing form. To the chagrin of many purists this often ends up creating an accommodative and hybrid version of the local culture. Though, with vast human migration, changing demographics, shrinking world there are not many true blue 'Mono-National' States left.

The more Poly-National a State gets, it would do good by functioning off a Constitution that is not strongly influenced by religious tenets. I am sure if a similar death, like that of Savita, would have happened to an Irish national, while equally condemnable, the news would have been restricted to the local media. However as we had a person of different nationality at the centre of such an event, the inadequacy of the Mono-Nation State's ability to move away from religious tenets or reluctance to accept the changing demographics comes to the fore. One would have thought that Church dominating the politics of land was a thing of Medieval ages, but looks like we were wrong.

Most of the rich Mono-National states had an issue of lack of sufficient college graduates with specific skills; this meant that to fill the gap they needed to import those skills from abroad where there was abundance of resources. Importing resources and hoping that they leave their culture back home is a rather Utopian dream. Hence flexibility and readiness to accept the changes is needed so that no more lives are lost. I think ***States are better off being religiously neutral***. This should also help one to understand and appreciate the complexity of running a poly-nation state like India.

# The Presidential Suite

## <u>19 *Monday* Nov 2012</u>

The dust has settled on the US presidential elections, finally to the relief or agony or many other contradictory feelings of people, a President is in place at the White House. As the frayed nerves are put at ease I wanted to share a few observations I had during the course of the campaign leading upto the elections and declaration of result.

**Firstly** Globalization should have meant that a part of the world is present in every other part of the world, like fractals. The exchange of information, cross cultural corporate environment and access to information via Internet or television should have made it easier for this to happen. What seems to have happened though, is that the World has got closer to USA rather than the other way around. *So events such as US Presidential elections are no longer watched and monitored only by US citizens but by many ordinary citizens, like me, world over.*

**Secondly,** while it is indeed amusing to see so much dinner time or cocktail party debates on US Presidential candidates in countries that are thousands of miles away from US, there is no doubt that the ***person who gets the job has an immediate effect on foreign policy involving these far off countries***. The policies of 'father Bush' administration or 'son Bush' administration or Obama administration has not only had repercussions on their own populace but in far off places like

Iraq, Iran, Israel, Afghanistan, Pakistan, India and China to name a few. Hence political leaders world over keep a close watch on the proceedings.

**Thirdly** *due to the strong ideology based politics US political parties are so easy to identify with*;. You have a set of belief about abortion, euthanasia, gay marriage or China or outsourcing, you automatically become part of one or the other political outfit.

**Fourth**, elections are, apart from everything else, also about money. The advertisements, the travel for campaigning, entourage, accommodation, dinners; all cost money. Wherever there is a question of money there is a high chance of misdoings and illegal methods for raising funds, US elections show, how it could be kept clean by *bringing in transparency into the funding process*. Everybody knows where all the money came from and tries and keeps it as clean as possible.

**Fifth**, *televised debates between the presidential candidates.* This, I think, is the hallmark of the US Presidential elections. Two matured gentleman going hard at each other but with dignity, grace and entirely on the basis of facts, figures, policies and strategy. No raised voices, no rising temper, no backbiting. Everything in public view to live audiences, so everything is on record and available for repeated viewing and any goof ups or mistakes impossible to escape from.

**Sixth**, the *developing economies world over have nothing to learn directly from type of politics of US*. The situations are different, demographics are different hence these countries are better left to themselves to work on their own type of politics. Any attempt to blindly adopt some of the methods could lead to disastrous consequences.

**Seventh**, Last but definitely not the least, the biggest learning for all is about *grace in defeat and humility in victory*. Romney and Obama both demonstrated this perfectly, one conceding defeat without losing dignity and the other claiming victory without being condescending

# Looking East and Seeing West

## <u>16 *Tuesday* Oct 2012</u>

We all know that corruption is not a new phenomenon. documented evidences of corruption have been found in the mythological epics of most of the parts of the world. Corruption continues to be in limelight, probably more in the developing economies of the East than the developed ones of the West. Infact the picture often painted with respect to corruption is, that of a Clean West and a chaotic, murky and Corrupt East.

Corruption, like many other things, is tough to define in definite terms. For the sake of simplicity we would limit the scope here to, offerings of cash and kind in order to gain personal benefits. This is the most widely recognised and experienced form of corruption. I want to point out here that, while the developing countries of the east are seeing rapid increase of corrupt practices, the west cannot claim any moral superiority over the matter. On the contrary West has long been known for finding innovative ways to continue corrupt practices yet make it look clean and transparent on the outside. Also, the results of such corrupt practices are far reaching and affect millions way beyond the boundaries of country where they are perpetrated. It is a known fact now that, the West at large had almost legalised methods of corruption and conveniently gave it the name of Lobbying. Lobbying as a concept had existed from early 19th century and became more prevalent and popular post The Great Depression of

1938. The so called Cartels [Oil, Weapon, Pharmaceuticals etc.] appointed lobbyists to influence Senators/Congressmen/Parliamentarians and get favorable legislations passed in the Congress/Parliament. Benefits were mutual, the Cartels got benefits like

- **Lower taxes**
- **Ability to bribe officials to gain contracts in other countries and claim tax benefit on it in their country of origin**
- **Gain Overseas and Domestic Government Contracts**
- **Lower interest rates for Loans**
- **Prevent unfavorable laws from being legislated**

Every favor done to the respective Cartels, the legislators got either

- **Election Funds**
- **Party Funds**
- **An Influential position in Private Sector**

One would argue that in the East corruption impacts ordinary people and in the West it is restricted to the upper echelons of the power equation. One could also argue that in the East we have to bribe even if we have to obtain a birth certificate, whereas in the West such hassles don't exist. Here I would like to present some facts that would indicate how debilitating the corrupt practices of west could be, way beyond the affect of corruption that the East sees from day to day.

- **The strong lobbying of the rich and influential in the USA has ensured very low taxes for them** compared to the middle class, often referred by Warren Buffet as key point to look into. Thus increasing the tax burden on ordinary people to meet the deficit and fund Government expenditure

- **Strong lobbying by the Banks ensured near 0% interest rates and almost free supply of money across the world leading to an indiscreet granting of loans starting early 2000. It also ensured removal of regulations on banking and mortgages which led to the bloodbath of 2008, the ripple effects of which are still being felt.**
- **Strong lobbying by Banks ensured huge bailout packages at the expense of tax payers money leading to huge fiscal deficit, meaning reduced spending by Government on essential health care and other social benefits leading to job losses, reduced family income and expensive health care.**
- **Strong lobbying by Oil companies allowed BP to construct a reservoir with substandard material that eventually led to the oil spill and vast damage to the ecosystem.**

All of the above have had far reaching affect on not only the common man in the country where it originated but have spread to shores far beyond as a domino effect. The damage done is much more severe than what paying for a birth certificate could be. Doesn't this smell like the same rotten stuff that one often associates with the East? Why then, do we perceive the West as more cleaner than the East? Aren't they in the same rut as us? Aren't we in a way suffering for corrupt practices committed way beyond our own shores?

Ofcourse I am not justifying the corrupt practices of the east or indicating that it is better than that of the west.

Both are equally condemnable and possibly tough to get rid of. There might be some merit in the thought of legalising corruption and make it as transparent as possible. This is what the West has done and hence continues to be ranked high up in the Transparency International's Corruption Perception Index. Ofcourse the East has to deal with other factors, like literacy levels, before it could make any change in how the world perceives it.

# Crisis Zone

## <u>15 *Monday* Oct 2012</u>

The Euro Zone is probably fighting the gravest battle since the time it was conceived by members of the European Union (EU). Euro was introduced around 1999 as a currency that could be used across all the EU member countries. Soon it was proposed to replace the local currency of each of the member country. Over a span of 10 years, 17 of the 27 EU countries changed their local currency to the Euro. The rationale behind such a dramatic move was to

- Increase trade collaboration within the EU member countries
- Reduce dependency on US $ to influence the exchange rate fluctuation
- Increased cross border employment opportunity
- Better cost parity across countries
- Opportunity for, the developing economies in the EU to restructure their economic fundamentals and pave way for growth

Euro today is only second to the US $ in terms of net worth and the currency in which global trade is being carried out. Also to a large extent it has managed to make itself immune from the number of $ in circulation, ofcourse a 100% immunity is neither possible nor desired. So all the

17 countries that agreed to convert to Euro soon came to be known as The Euro-Zone. Interestingly though, UK is not among the 17 countries, though Euro is accepted as a currency for trade but the Pound still remains their local currency.

Whatever limited success that Euro has enjoyed till date, it is quite interesting to note that there was one key inherent flaw. The flaw was that, there was a common monetary policy across the Euro-zone countries but there was no common fiscal policy across them. This meant that while it was understood by the Governments what currency they are dealing with and how much of it, there was no understanding about how each Government was spending them. It isn't like the United States or India where, while each state makes their own independent decision on State Government expenditure but it is still within the framework of the Central Government. With the lack of such over-viewing body, each country had it's own fiscal policy and went ahead and did whatever they thought was best for their people without realising that how it would affect other countries.

Governments in most countries tend to spend on infrastructure to generate jobs in public sector, provide unemployment benefits and some of them offer pensions and other social benefits. These expenditures are to be funded.

A. **You could print money to fund them (at the risk of inflation)**
B. **You could increase taxes (income/sales/service/ excise/customs) and increase revenue (to the dissatisfaction of people)**
C. **You could borrow money against Government bonds (with risk of higher fiscal deficit).**

All said and done the option that least impacted people immediately was borrowing money, hence lot of countries like Greece were known to have large fiscal deficit and used to borrow heavily to fund their social benefits programs. Individual countries making their own decision to provide benefit to their own people in the Euro Zone was interestingly coming at the expense of every other country also part of the same Euro Zone. Amidst this came the economic slow down of 2008 and what was worse was that banks were failing and falling like dry leaves. Even central banks of some countries lost their stability. There was only two options – allow the banks to fail or recapitalise the banks by injecting genuine (and not speculative) funds into them. The vote was in favor of injecting funds and billions of Euro's were offered as bail out packages to these banks as they were seen as a the back bone of the economy and their failing or falling could lead to horrible bloodbath. This sort of paved way for more such stimulus funds or packages which has only made the matter worse.

With a linked currency, what it meant now was a country's exports or imports could become expensive or cheap depending upon the exchange rate of the Euro. Greece suffered the consequences of this and suddenly found them in a position where their exports became expensive to buy and imports became expensive to sustain, thus further fueling their debt levels. Most countries like Greece or Spain, in order to raise money sold Government bonds to other countries and borrowed heavily, which meant that all the countries that bought these bonds became dependent directly on the well-being of these countries. It is a catch 22 situation all the way. Let me explain.

- **Countries like Greece or Spain have borrowed so heavily that they can continue to sustain only if they can still borrow; even if it means that their bonds are of no value. Which means the other countries have to suffer losses to sustain Greece**

- **There is a need to politically influence countries like Greece or Spain to reduce their respective public spending**
- **Reduced public spending would mean loss of jobs and incomes for households which would mean either higher unemployment benefit cost again leading to debt or reduced collection of tax and a shrinking GDP**
- **One could ask why not let Greece drop out of the Euro Zone and revert back to it's old currency, well what about the bonds they sold to other countries? What worth would they be? What value will they get, indirectly it influences the financial stability of countries who bought these bonds**

Not an easy decision to make, however what the Euro-zone Political leaders have agreed upon is inline with the problem we highlighted above

- Write off some part of Debts (non-repayment of loans), especially Greece
- Offer bailout package to sustain the countries
- Resort to AUSTERITY – a move popularised and strongly voiced by German Chancellor Angela Merkel – basically means reduced Government spending on social benefits and other activities to ensure the debts don't increase dramatically.

It looks to be a fair decision provided, saving the Euro-Zone is a predetermined objective. Hence I said at the beginning it is the gravest battle that Euro-zone is fighting for it's own survival. The country that could probably be smiling with a 'I told you So' smile is UK, who have remained relatively immune to this turmoil and ofcouse so have been the 9 other EU members who decided to stay out of the Euro-Zone. The Political and Economic big-wigs of Europe are definitely making an all out effort to keep alive their baby (the Euro Zone) however, it is coming at an expense of competitiveness of individual countries to sustain and earn their way out of crisis.

If Greece is allowed to fall out of the Euro Zone they could devalue their currency which would make their exports cheaper and imports sustainable. This would aid them to earn greater returns from exports helping to minimise fiscal deficit. It would give them the opportunity to revive their economic health and rejoin Euro-Zone when in a better shape. Holding other countries contingent to Greece is like telling me that, how much I can spend today is dependent on how much my neighbor already spent yesterday. Because of Greece all other countries which are part of Euro Zone are now in the AUSTERITY mode which means reduced public spending. This has led to public outcry, loss of jobs, emotional turmoil, depression, suicides and many other repercussions of it. If Euro Zone has to be sustained the turmoil and disturbance is inevitable, infact leaders would like us to believe that the turmoil is only a trade-off for a long term benefit. However there are other options that could be explored if so desired.

This is the thing about Globalization, today nobody is entirely immune from what goes on in the other parts of the world. So if global economy has to recover, EU and Euro Zone play a crucial role in it. Hence their well-being is as important as any.

# Lance Around

## <u>12 *Friday* Oct 2012</u>

'What a fall was there, my countrymen' said Mark Antony about the death of Julius Caesar. The expression of the world towards Lance Armstrong is no different today.

Lance Armstrong was among those sporting icons who had managed to get fame beyond the boundaries of his own country and well beyond the followers of the sport that he patronized. He gave hope to people suffering from cancer as he fought against the disease and came back successfully to win series of Tour De France crown. Some of us might remember the yellow Livestrong bracelets that, both in it's original and counterfeit form, had become widely popular across the world and were symbols of wide spread support for people fighting against cancer. Yet here is the man facing the most severest charges that would make people who trusted in him feel ashamed of. US Anti-Doping Agency (USADA) indicates it has more than a strong case against Armstrong. With each passing day more and more of his former team mates are coming out with their own accounts of how they were bullied and coerced to fall in line with the doping practices prescribed by Lance Armstrong.

Whether he would come out of these allegations that are yet to be proved, remains to be seen. However there is no denying his skills as a cyclist that he demonstrated very early in his life though the doping charges threaten to completely obliterate his skills as a cyclist. It is essential to note that the charges against him start from year 1999, by then he was already an established professional cyclist winning many competitions and races in the US and Europe. He won two Tour De Force titles in 1993 (Stage 8) and 1995 (Stage 18). It was in 1996 that he was diagnosed with Testicular cancer. The big blotch though is that his famous wins at Tour De France, post his recovery from cancer, came within the years where he is alleged to have been deep into taking performance enhancement drugs, thus raising credibility about how much of his success could be attributed to his spirit and how much to the performance enhancement drugs. Can personal greed push one to such extreme acts?

Sporting standards have undoubtedly gone many notches higher. While the human body hasn't evolved in any visible sense yet year over year athletes have improved dramatically and give performances that almost seem nonhuman-like. Most of the athletes and sportsmen (Cricket or Football) seem to play almost all through out the year defying the wear and tear of the body, swimmers and sprinters continue to better the event records. This doping allegation against Lance Armstrong raises fingers against all sporting icons in all fields! It leaves one with a sense of fear who the next sporting great could be, ready to fall from grace? How many of the performances that we have admired in various sports are the result of performance enhancement drugs? Are all the sportsmen adept in knowing how to take drugs and not get caught (less adept do get caught)? How much of a success in an event can be attributed to the athletes skills and how much to the enhancement from drugs?

It is scary to imagine if sports has become like a Daily Soap, playing to the needs of the viewers. What if sports was to be played out with predetermined scripts that get tweaked depending on what viewers want (betting scandal is already known)? Does the sport influence the viewer-ship or is the viewer-ship influencing the sport? Fate of Lance Armstrong would soon be decided; however I hope that it acts as a wakeup call for many others in case if any have resorted to similar means. Criminal act of any nature and type never pays; it does come back to haunt the perpetrator one way or the other

# Too Much of Government is bad for Economic Health

## <u>27 _Thursday_ **Sep 2012**</u>

Governments, world over, are accepted and respected. Today we don't spare time to think how Governments came into existence and who gave them the right to make rules and tax people. Infact today we accept the legitimacy of Government, so much so that we entrust it with lot of responsibilities and believe that it acts in the best interest of the people. After the 2008 economic depression, Governments have become stronger than ever. Governments now control finances and operations of many financial institutions. With the severe repercussion that people had to face in some of the liberalised economies, people are ready to willingly accept the domination and increased interference from Governments in exchange for stability.

While the knee jerk reaction of people who, suffered or are still suffer the fall out of the economic crisis is understandable, yet it is essential for all of us to understand that over sized Government, interfering in daily economic activities reduces our income level and leads to financial instability than the other way round. Lot of Keynesian economist would like to believe that the Government should spend their way out of any economic crisis, this sentiment also gets echoed in some of the Asian countries where there is a large reliance on Government for jobs and infrastructural development. However research conducted by economist in leading universities of the world and independent bodies don't agree with this view point.

Let us examine. The sources of Government revenue are one of the following:

- Direct and Indirect Taxes [Custom duty | Excise Duty | Sales Tax | Service Tax| Income Tax etc,]
- Profits from Public Sector Units [PSU]
- Influencing Central Banks [ex: Federal Reserve in US] to print money
- Borrowings from International markets against Government Bonds

If the Government has to increase spending it has to fund that spending through revenue from one or a mix of the above available sources. Let us see the repercussion of using any of these instruments:

**Taxes:** If the Government funds it's spending through increasing taxes, everyone earns lesser and have lower disposable income to spend. Private Sector companies might be encouraged to increase prices to meet their earning targets thus affected sales. The people are encouraged to report their income falsely so they could pay lesser tax and this leads to creation of black money.

**Profits from PSU:** There are very few PSU in the world that are making profit, the one that are making profit are not at par with the private sector with respect to infrastructure or technology. Tremendous investment is required to bring them up to the level where they could continue to compete with private players and remain profitable for long time. This is not possible if the Government eats into their profits to fund some project that doesn't have direct influence on the PSU's own business.

**Printing Money:** It is well established now that printing excess money than what an economy can handle leads to inflation as there is suddenly more money chasing same amount of Products and Services. Inflation reduces value or the net worth of our savings and strongly effects consumer sentiments and Institutional investors alike

**Borrowings against Government Bonds:** Borrowings for a short durations seem to be a good option, though excess borrowing increases the fiscal deficit (public debt). Higher public debt is sign of an unstable economy and is unsustainable for a long run. Research shows that increase in public debt has a negative influence on the GDP.

Though as a practice a combination of the above sources has often been used by majority of the Governments across the world to fund their expenditure. It has had limited success and created more problems than it managed to solve. The European crisis (Euro zone Crisis) is one such example where excess spending by Governments of member countries of the EU that, had the same currency, has led to severe instability. So the larger a role we want Government to play, the larger their employee base and larger the need to fund their human resources and functions, larger would be their reliance on using or misusing one or multiple of the above sources available at their disposal.

I would like to argue that, lesser the Government more would be the benefit to the ordinary man. Having said that,

I am still am in favor of a minimal Government as a vigilante that keeps an eye on economic activity and the economic institutions to ensure stability to prevent unhealthy and speculative investment decisions. It should play a constructive role in making it attractive for private local and international players to invest in countries infrastructure. Governments could continue to play role in ensuring Literacy, minimum education level, minimum nutrition levels and facilitate it as much as possible thus playing a constructive role in ensuring roadblocks to do business are removed. Create level playing field to ensure fair competition, be the implementer of law. People have to feel empowered and given empowerment to use their entrepreneurial spirit to start businesses and be nurtured by favorable conditions to expand.

# Corruptible Ideals

## 15 *Saturday* Sep 2012

Circa 2011 – 2012 will probably go down in History as the era of Protests and Changes. The 12-18 months time frame we talk about has been a witness to some ocean of changes inspired by public outcry and protests. One such protest, among many, has been the Anti-Corruption/LokPal Bill movement in India. Initiated and inspired by the unflinching energy of Anna Hazare, it went on to gain public attention and also led to the formation of, what we now know as, Team Anna.

Inspite of all the public support, countrywide protests and oceans of people gathering at various places in the country not much has been achieved not much has been changed. This is contrary to what we saw in the Arab Spring uprisings. Why has this movement only become a Team Anna movement? Why was it not a Indian Mass Movement? Why did it fail to meet it's desired goal? Why did it have limited success leading to reduced response and lesser crowds as the protest progressed?

There are few basic facts that I think contributed to this:

- Discounting the fact that a majority of the politicians had won their elections fair and square
- Assuming that if they name their organization – India Against Corruption, that would automatically mean the whole country is with them

- Failing to understand that no single Org can ever claim to be the true representative of the entire Nation-state of India, if anybody does so it would remain just that, Claim and far from reality
- Not Defining Corruption – Corruption is a vague term, there are various types of corruption which includes Moral as well. So the scope of the protest was never announced
- Last but not the least is the utter dis-respect to the Constitution of Indian Union

**Compare this with the Arab Spring, large scale success as the objective of the movement were very clear to the protestors and their supporters and the results for all of us to see.**

If we treat IAC as a party then I could say that the people did accept Anna Hazare as the PM candidate from IAC but the same people could not give them the mandate as the party's agenda wasn't clear. I have never seen a leader who is as confused as Arvind Kejriwal. Most of the protests in India tend to be Socialist in their nature. This inspite of the fact that Nehru's socialist dream failed to give the country what it was promised. Mr Kejriwal's resignation from Civil Service, simple attire, sleeping on the floor all give an impression of a socialist movement, which is scary. Every statement that Mr Kerjiwal comes out with gives an impression that he would like to re-write the constitution of the country and start everything from scratch. Lot of people would like that, but the reality is that we need to start from wherever we are, whatever we are and move. While his intent may not be wrong but I am sorry to say the approach and the execution are rather childish.

It looks like finally Mr Kejriwal has understood that the battle has to be fought within the framework of the constitution. He announced formation of a political party on the 2nd October 2012 under his leadership (minus Anna) and indicates their prime aim would be to give the power back to the people. There is, as per me, lot of rhetoric but very less practical sense in the vision statement he put forward and the methodologies that he propose have tinge of extremism and importantly socialism written all over it. No matter what Mr Kejriwal wants to call it, from economic point of view it looks like an attempt to go the Marxist way and politically it looks to be rather naive. Nonetheless only time will tell if he gains the trust and support of the people he believes he represents and can his party remain clean inspite of being inside the system

# Humor

# The Circus of Indian Marriage

## <u>18 *Tuesday* Sep 2012</u>

Marriage in anybody's life is quite a landmark and once in a lifetime event. It is something that all look forward to albeit, some with fear and anxiety, some with hope and excitement. In India, some might observe, the life revolves around marriages. Either people are busy searching for a bride/groom or people are busy attending marriages or busy arranging marriages or busy pestering an unmarried guy or a girl to submission and agree for marriage. If you are on the wrong side of 30 and unmarried then, no matter where you go, whether official or personal discussions eventually the topic changes to 'when are you getting married', add to it a questioning look of 'is there something wrong with you'?

While this is an unaccepted and unacknowledged fact that life for a lot of people in India revolves around marriages, what is also true is that Marriages in India are complicated and the complexity of marriages has only increased over time. The complexity is not as much in the marriage itself (though that exists too), it is more in the build-up to the marriage. India, to a large extent, has come out of the parochial view point of casteism and religious divide. Atleast in the urban landscape and corporate world the Indian Middle Class has learnt to look at a unified merit based society, rather than viewing it with caste based hierarchy. Yet, one situation which brings out this divide more strongly than anything else is while deciding on a partner for marriage. Here, all Indians go back to their own caste based and religion based cocoons, almost like a sheepish sudden realisation!

Indian marriages could be classified under two large categories, Arranged Marriages and Love Marriages. Arranged is where parents find a bride or groom for their wards and solemnise the marriage and they live happily ever after. Love is where the girl and guy mutually agree that they are right for each other and decide to marry sometimes solemnised by parents sometimes not.

With whatever minimal savings I have, I would still like to risk betting that finding a life partner in India is the toughest task than anywhere else in the world. This, even without having to touch upon 'matching wavelength', 'similar likes or dislikes' and all the jazz involved in choosing a life partner.

There are some essential filters that a person has to cross before he or she could be considered as a possible partner. First is Religion, you have to be of the same religion; Second is Caste, you have to be of the same caste, some might feel that this is too less a complication for a simple life and might want to go to the micro level of particular sub-caste; Third is Language, you need to speak the same language. Yes you could be of the same religion and caste however, what fun is it if you abuse in a language that your partner and family won't understand at all. Fourth is food habits, veg or non-veg? Fifth is Astrology, most families with varying degree, on what Astrology says. Sometimes even more than their own common sense or rational decision making. Sixth is Education/Salary- should earn sufficient for maintaining a family. Seventh – Job type, and Eighth – Looks, well atleast they should be bearable to look at, ain't it?

Knowing the type of marriages in India and the requirements, am sure one would like to think that Arranged marriages should be easy. Parents just follow the filtering process and present the final result to the marriage ready ward and finalise. Well it is definitely not as easy as it sounds to be, firstly post Independence, India did notice some migration within the country. So there are many instances where a family settles for decades together in a Province which they don't belong to. There are not many of their own type in the Province where they are settled and might have lost touch with people of their own Province and find it tough to find someone who could qualify all the filters or majority of the filters. Another big factor that has added to the complication is Women's Liberation. No I am not a misogynist. Women's Liberation meant that Indian women were getting educated and as in most occasions devoid of pressure of maintaining a household (exceptions do exist), getting very highly educated. So even if all the filters mentioned above match, now comes additional complications, Salary – should earn more than her, Job type – should be mentionable, Education – should be more educated than her, Life Style – few overseas trips and holiday in Thailand, English – should be fluent and so on and so forth.

If Arranged could get complicated like what I mention above, you could very well imagine how severely complicated could Love Marriages get. There are various permutation and combination among the basic requirements which would not pass the filter test. I will give just one example. Yes you are from same religion, yes you are from same caste but, you don't speak the same language. How would you communicate with respective families, what language would you speak with each other all your life? What language would your kid speak?. I guess by now you are well equipped to think of much more complicated situations and could spend hours at it as well. The more India develops the more people migrate to other states in search of better job opportunities and meet people from various backgrounds, it is only more likely that now we see such complicated relations emerging more often than not.

Having said what I have said so far, Marriages do happen in India both love marriages and arranged marriages and happen in large numbers. Marriage as an institution has not lost it's hold on the society and continues to be an essential aspect of Indian life. At this point we are not even questioning which form of marriages lead to more happier marriages, nor am I any authority to be able to comment on it. I only wanted to bring out the complications involved in deciding on a life partner in the Indian context. There are more aspects which I haven't touched upon for simplicity sake, however might come back to at a later stage.

# The Facebook Celebrity

I guess, most of us have tried to imagine how the life of a celebrity would be. The stardom, the recognition, people jostling with each other to catch a glimpse, rushing to get an autograph and the various other things that come with being a celebrity. It is ofcourse restricted to a fortunate (for lack of a better word) few.

For the rest of the unfortunate (again for the lack of a better word) many, having vicarious experiences while day dreaming or reading magazines and newspapers is the only last resort. It looks like, if there is a God somewhere or of some type he did listen to the voices of the unfortunate many. Out of no where comes a Harvard Uni student and builds an App that would change the lives of most of the unfortunate many and challenge the status of the fortunate few. Yes I am talking about Mark Zuckerberg and Facebook. I don't find it surprising at all that Mark was majoring in Computer Science and Psychology when attending the University. He definitely understood the psyche of his target audience and developed something that catered to the inadequacy of the unfortunate many,

Facebook is going great guns, for most of us, the day is not complete without paying few visits to the site. For some, Facebook is THE work for which they come to office for and they do the other job just to sustain their THE work. Some we notice suffering from an Obsessive Compulsive Behavior (OCB) of sharing photographs no matter what they do. I will bet half my salary (peanuts as it may be) on saying that sales of SLR cameras and the associated lenses have never been as good as it is now after the advent of Facebook. In a way it seems to have made people realise their dormant talent and also this incessant desire to share it with people. Silently all this has created something that definitely hasn't gone unnoticed but most of the time goes unmentioned. It has created something called a Facebook Celebrity.

The Facebook Celebrity (FBC) is not as much of a person as it is a feeling. It is attached to the number of LIKES or COMMENTS received on a post or an album or a photograph or a status change. Ofcourse there is a gender bias. Posts or Photographs of Ladies tend to see a stampede of people rushing to hit the Like button or comment, Posts or Photographs of Gents sometimes don't tend to find much of an audience (not even a fly). Ofcourse there is a status bias, Posts or Photographs of Sr Managers in any organization witnesses another stampede of subordinates and colleagues trying to outdo each other in innovative comments apart from hitting the Like button. I am still not sure if this has started influencing the annual performance review nonetheless it is a phenomenon to be observed. So what this has created is that feeling of being a celebrity or knowing what does it feel like to be a celebrity; where every move and every act is watched by many. The beautify of FBC is that it could be anyone of us, I am sure many of us have sensed this feeling and know that it is very democratic and allows anyone to be have that feeling.

As with many other things, this FBC thing is not without it's own pitfalls or repercussions. It is nothing different than the highs and lows stars see linked with their performances in their respective profession. People have reported psychological disorders linked to responses on their Facebook posts, some have reported severe depression when their postings don't get any likes or not as many likes as they expected there to be, some have reported sleepless nights when a profile picture change didn't evoke any response and were tempted to take botox. It has blurred the lines of private and public. Private boozing sessions at a friends place is now meant to be public knowledge and photographs published all over the place with elan are a norm, or a silent dinner with family is meant to be public knowledge and probably the food doesn't digest well unless some pics landup on the Facebook site. Such is the entrapment of a FBC.

Nonetheless it has definitely done one thing it has, in a way, brought the unfortunate many at par with the fortunate few and has made it a 'passing the ball' game as far as the FBC feeling is concerned. Yes the fortunate few still continue to get millions of views but the unfortunate many with hundreds or thousands of views don't feel any less important. It is definitely also removing the way society views certain professions and bringing them at par with the respected others, though the paychecks are not in a hurry to level themselves out, nonetheless the bias to some extent is going away. So I think the FBC phenomenon is here to say inspite of the many pitfalls it has and make a STAR out of all of us.

Three Cheers to FBC

# Shoe – Silence Please

I think all of us remember the incident where Bush had a pair of shoes hurled at him in Baghdad. Ever since that incident there have been flurry of incidents across the world where shoes were thrown at politicians. Wonder if anybody spared a thought about why it caught up like a craze and spread like forest fire as a mode of protest.

I know there might be different theories to explain this; however I think the reason is more apolitical. The shoes that were thrown, I think, were those which made the most embarrassing of noises while walking on the office floor. In other words these must have been farting shoes that are an embarrassment to the wearer. I have been victim of such shoes which look smart and are extremely comfortable but have a strange knack of making odd noises when walking in office. Each time I found myself in such awkward situation I wished I could walk barefoot, wished I could vanish, wished I didn't have to walk much, hoped magically the noise would stop. However I never thought that I could use it to throw at people that I didn't like and not only get rid of my problem but also gain some popularity in the bargain.

Looking at the string of shoe throwing incidents across the world I realize that I am not only one who faces the problem of noisy shoes. However, while mine sneer at me sitting on my shoe shelf, other's had the distinction of flying over popular politician's head! One must also observe that in all such shoe throwing incidents the shoe never hit the person it was hurled at, it swooshes past but never ever has it hit. Why would it? If you could make your mark and fulfill your objective without hitting the target, why bother to waste extra time. Shoe companies or showrooms are not making any extra effort in ensuring that people could wear and trial shoes on a surface that closely resembles their office floor in texture so, I wouldn't be surprised if we see a continuance of people at the tether end of their patience with their farting shoes and let go their frustration on the shoe and the politician in one go and for the same reason.

# Dumb and Dumber

## 21 _Monday_ Jan 2013

For a change I am in a country where you don't have to convert every cost into $, everything is in $! I am in a country where things are done in brazenly different manner than rest of  the world. Switches work the other way, weight is measured in pounds, distance measured in miles, petrol is called gasoline and measured in gallon and so on and so forth. As a friend once painstakingly pointed out, everything done, in order to do away from colonial past and create a completely new Identity. Thank fully they couldn't do much with time; it is still 60 seconds a minute and 60 minutes an hour. Nonetheless It's a very 'politically aware' nation and as I write this blog – TV is all about Obama's swearing in for his second innings at the White house.

There is one more thing that one would obviously notice, something that I have started to hate, driving! Yes as everything else, they drive on the other side, which they call the right side! The steering wheel is on the other side as well! After a day that, it takes for 'getting used' it is quite a dumbing down experience to drive here. I have been driving for the last three days here – weigh what sort of stress I have been put through:

- I don't need to decide the appropriate gear
- I don't need to preempt the worst the guy in front would do
- I don't need to worry about how to avoid scratches on the car
- I don't need to worry about the car rolling back
- I don't need to worry about how to maneuver around junctions with no signals
- I don't need to worry about finding out how to squeeze between two vehicles
- I don't need to worry about how to intimidate drivers around me to submission
- I don't need to indicate in absolute certain terms that I want to turn right or left
- I don't need to decide whether I need to stop at a signal or speed up
- I don't need to honk at anyone for anything

I fear if I continue driving in this country a few more days not only will I find it tough once I am back where I belong, but also my IQ would have fallen a good 50 points. Changing from survival of the fittest to 'live and let live' is stressful and comes with its own pitfalls of lower intelligence! Choose- intelligence or Driving Comfort? Don't blame me if I look dumb in the picture! A dear friend asked me – 'which one is dumb' and 'which one is dumber'? Be your own judge!

# Dearer Endearment

God and Inflation. One might wonder what the two have to do with each other. Some might think that it is about God helping us dealing with inflation. No, I have something else in mind. All religions prescribe some way or the other to help us take our requests to God and also ask us to nurture hope of getting our requests accepted and answered. Have we ever thought of how much the price of such requests have gone up over the past few years? How much burden of inflation do we have to suffer to reach the omniscient?

Long ago when population was less and things cheaper, I would assume, it would have been easier to get attention and requests fulfilled. Whether it is an offering [candles, oil, fruits, sweets etc.] or whether it is a pilgrimage it has only become costlier to be heard and seek the blessing of the almighty. Often it is also the satisfaction of a priest that decides the satisfaction in the rituals performed and possibly satisfaction of the worshipped deity, here also what used to suffice few years ago is considered a pittance today. Not so long ago, a friend asked if 'priests were beggars'? If we don't treat what priests do as a service and don't consider it to in anyway help us get ourselves closer to God or be heard by God, well then, they are possibly beggars in disguise! So are all of us who also believe that we offer some service that is worthy enough to earn us our money.

Some might argue that to keep pace with inflation both the quantity and quality of offerings have suffered. Then the question is whether we have found yet another shortcut to keep the almighty happy for less? Some might also argue that it is not in the offerings but the honesty of feelings behind the offering that matters. I don't know any way to measure the honesty behind offerings nor do I know how it has changed over time. Though, offerings do tend to keep track with changes in earning capability but not essentially with inflation. It appears more of a subjective interpretation of what we assume to be sufficient to please and get the desired result, rather than what possibly is demanded of. How would we know what is demanded off anyway!

However inflation in these matters is not entirely avoidable. Installing deities at home, offerings, pilgrimages all have become dearer than before so much so that some can't afford it. Behind all this is wisdom. Whatever wisdom is available at our disposal constantly makes this active choice of how much, how often, worth of it, whether desired results are met. Is God at the mercy of our individual wisdom or is our wisdom at the mercy of God – it is for people to observe.

# Destructive Upgrade

Have you ever lost a mobile phone? It is tough to get through life without losing one I guess! Those who have lost their mobile phones should be able to identify with a sinking feeling that gushes in immediately after we realize that we have indeed lost our mobile. Ofcourse the feeling dawns only after we are exhausted from frantic attempts to trace the mobile and from innumerable calls that we make to our own number with a hope that somebody would answer and miraculously we get our mobile back. Such situations do happen albeit rarely so. Immediate aftermath of such exhausting exercise is the sting of the truth sinking in –yes the mobile is lost – this is when feelings take over with a sense of nostalgia and proud memories of what was achieved with the great device. Often mobile phones are given as gifts, so there are emotions attached to the device and loss of a gift also brings a sense of guilt. Ofcourse the most painful of pinch is felt when an expensive, brand new mobile with latest feature is lost or stolen. Like any other pain this settles down too.

Once the feelings settle down and the bitter truth is accepted, comes a sense of relief. Relief that stems from knowing that we can always get a new phone (maybe latest one), a SIM card can be reissued for the same number, all the phone numbers, of friends or relatives, could be retrieved from any of the social networking sites through which we are in touch with all or most. Whoever is not there on any of these sites and whose number we can't retrieve were anyway insignificant or people who needed us more than we needed them.

Not much data is available on the internet to substantiate if loss of mobile is one of the primary reasons why someone thinks of buying a new phone. A general understanding of the matter led me to two other reasons:

- • - Current one stopped working – out of order
- • - Genuine interest to keep pace with emerging technology trends and features

And

- • - Loss of the current one [misplaced or stolen]

Am sure that, except for a few that are hard core techies and love technology rest wait for an unfortunate incident of loss or fatal failure of a mobile before they could be coaxed to buy one.

# Facebook Dire-Rear

## **18** *Saturday* **May 2013**

Facebook, in the few years of its existence, has almost become an essential aspect of most people's lives. There are many uninitiated and uninterested people who today are converts and now well within the folds of Facebook and thus help increase its popularity even further. Infact, I read somewhere that, Facebook has sufficient members to be declared as a country!

On an earlier occasion I wrote about an emerging phenomenon called, Facebook Celebrity and the repercussions of being or not being one! Today I wanted to explore another such emerging phenomenon. I prefer to call this phenomenon Facebook Diarrhea. Pardon me for a slightly corny name to this phenomenon; I think no other name would have suited this behavior better. Diarrhea, as we all know, has symptoms of having three or more liquid bowel movements per day. Undoubtedly a serious condition and could be fatal as well.

Ofcourse the word Diarrhea, apart from being used to describe a medical condition, has been used in more occasions than one to describe similar liquid movements of things other than just the bowel. For example a terminology used often to describe people who demonstrate symptoms of uncontrollable nonstop nonsense is, Verbal Diarrhea. Needless to say, the people at receiving end don't consider it to be a compliment and often take offense to it. Obviously I am fully aware that while describing a certain behavior and naming it Facebook diarrhea, I will be rubbing few people the wrong way and also be at the receiving end of their wrath. Nonetheless describe I will.

So, what is Facebook Diarrhea? A person suffering from this phenomenon demonstrates the following symptom: comes online (usually 3 or 4 times a day) and is in the grip of, a perpetual and uncontrollable, need to share and post on Facebook. So the person doesn't share just a single post, but shares a series of related or unrelated content (possibly timed by a stopwatch). I am sure, most of us have experienced this. When we login to our Facebook page, the Facebook wall is full of an almost never ending list of pictures, videos, posters and quotes shared by this individual. There is a liquid hand movement to hit the like and share button at whatever appears in sight. Unable to comprehend what makes such people stop I conclude that this behavior is stopwatched to a down count. I don't think an anti-dote has been found yet for Facebook Diarrhea.

One might ask why I don't pick Twitter. Twitter, if one observes, is all about diarrhea and it is the rule not the exception. So Twitter diarrhea cannot be described as a special phenomenon. There is many more such phenomenon waiting to be discovered on Facebook. Till I discover another one- so long.

# The Stare-Case

I always wondered, how long one could stare at a person without crossing any imaginary civilized boundary? More often than not, we walk across somebody who seems familiar but we immediately can't recollect and need to visually gather more information before any memory recall happens. The time needed to gather more visual information could vary and that would mean for whole of that duration either one is staring at the person in question or is stealing glances at him or her.

Wonder if there are acceptable time Also we definitely want to save ourselves the embarrassment of greeting somebody who ends up being a close resemblance only of somebody we know. Needless to say that, I am not referring to people who use this as a ploy to pursue their love interest! Limits that we draw intuitively so that the stare does not cross-over to a lecherous domain or to the domain of 'being interested'.

But really, is there a mental limit that we have beyond which the stare we receive or give becomes uncomfortable, threatening and intrusive? Does it vary culturally? I know not! All I know is that I have shot myself in the foot few times.

In a friends marriage I saw couple of faces that I thought were very familiar to me. They didn't show any indication of recognizing me, I had to look hard and try and gather as much visual details to confirm that these definitely were the ones that I know. I probably did it to an extent where the couple started showing some irritation. I had two option either stop staring, concentrate on my food and leave with the doubt permanently in my mind or to walk up to them with courage and ask if they could recognize me. For whatever reasons, I chose the latter! I walked upto them, stood before them with a smiling face and hoped that they would recognize me. They couldn't at all –I walked away a little embarrassed at the whole sequence of events. My friends, who saw me do this, thought that it was my habit to go upto strangers and ask if they recognized me!!

# Of Honkeys and Mutes

## <u>02 *Friday* Aug 2013</u>

Einstein said – **Two things are infinite: the universe and human stupidity and I am not sure about the universe!** There are umpteen real life examples to be seen on the road every day to prove Einstein right. Human stupidity is indeed infinite. The innovation that we can bring in the way we honk and in identifying situations that are worth a honk while driving/riding is unprecedented and unbridled display of human stupidity. In this display of stupidity there is no distinction of religion, caste, language, color, political inclination, rich or poor. Stupidity has the power in which it dissolves all individual identities and brings everyone to a level ground.

There are some typical stupid actions that are often linked with the habit of honking. Places which say 'No Horn' – 'School' – 'Hospital' somehow invite loudest of honk. Also some people consider themselves to be in a imagined computer game and the traffic congestion that they see ahead of them could be cleared with the weapon at their disposal – and a volley of laser beams is let lose – only difference though is that it doesn't really do anything to the traffic congestion in real life. Also most of us don't mind being stuck in the lives that we live for years together without doing anything different, yet the last 5 seconds at a red signal – somehow appears very worthy and worthy of some of the loudest and choicest of honks!

Infinite it is – stupidity – the quality and effectiveness of ones honking is somehow found related to the success in personal life. Good effective honking is also equated with a peaceful and gratifying day. Stupidity was proved infinite, almost conclusively, when one honked at a dead dog and another one at a fallen tree. Some of the compulsive honkers might want to fly and avoid all this congestion, but this is the thing, one can escape from traffic but not from stupidity so honking at the birds or the sun or the moon would be the norms. Hail Einstein!

# Bad-Men-In-Tons

People go to any extent to fulfill their passion and give meaning to their mundane life. Many have gone to the extent of even losing their lives in the pursuit of a passion. So here is the story of a group of friends with one such passion. While I would not say that anyone went to the extent of risking their lives, however risk they do and what they risk is by no means trivial.

Giving up the luxury of lazing in bed on the weekends they decide to pursue this passion and get the kicks on the field. Infact pursuing this passion could mean going home to an angry, irritated and cold shouldering spouse (could mean elongated stay of in-laws or no food or excessively long shopping list). Pursuing this passion could mean going home to irritated parents (could mean risking inheritance and paving the way towards the life of a pauper). Pursuing this passion could mean going home to annoyed kids (could mean risking long wish list, allowing equal time off from studies).

I guess by now one must have understood how much of a brave heart it takes to pursue this passion and I won't even count the physical readiness that it needs as that would appear a cake walk in front of the above risks. Yet risk they do and steal moments of bliss while losing themselves to their passion. What is this passion that one is willing to risk so much for? I talk about a beautiful game called Badminton.

Weekend after weekend people turn up to relieve themselves of all the stress of the past week, share a laugh, challenge each other on a game, discuss nuances of the game and also taunt each other on games lost or missed opportunities. People of disparate professional, cultural and linguistic background find a common ground to come together and sweat it out. The game has this unique ability of helping people to self-discover. Like some suddenly realize how unfit they are (all the running around, stretching and lunging can do that), some realize how good a liar they are (lying to spouse to spend extra minutes on the court needs such skills), some realize their misplaced priorities in life, many realize their ability to multi-task and many realize their limitations.

With such level of self-discovery one invariably reaches home enlightened to face any tough circumstances that the situation at home might throw up!!

# Screen Saver

<u>**21** *Friday* **Feb 2014**</u>

The Mobile phone, many would argue, was created to bring people closer with the place and time notwithstanding. Interestingly though the smartphone era is creating new barriers where none existed.

Mobile phones have invaded every aspect of our lives and they continue to extend the scope of what it could do for us. From being a simple phone it now is our point and shoot camera, organizer, personal PC, radio, music player, GPS device, gaming console and many more. Undoubtedly it still continues to be the device to call friends and be reached on.

So this device that was meant to breakdown barriers, how is it creating new ones? The answer lies in the behavior most of us might have either observed or demonstrated when faced with an unfavorable or uncomfortable situation. Typical example would be Lifts, Corridor, Public Transport or Public spaces. The 3.5" or more of smartphone screen provides sufficient space to hide and avoid eye contact or conversation in many situations, almost akin to cat drinking milk.

Want to avoid conversation with strangers, want to avoid conversation with people you don't like, want to avoid eye contact, forgot somebody's name, shy to start a conversation; lose yourself in the phone and create an invisible barrier that many would find tough to break. Adding a pair of headphones would further strengthen the invisible barrier almost making it impossible to breach for anyone.

So it is not uncommon now a days to see people getting into lift or public transport and instinctively reaching for their phone and tap the screen with focus and intent like there's a treasure waiting to be found. The moment they are out of the situation the phone would be promptly put away like a hot trail gone cold. So, there was this guy, regular to the gym I go. He would come to the gym and immediately take out his phone and start searching for something. His favorite exercise machine was the stationary cycle as that allowed him the option to continue to search for whatever he wanted to search on his phone while burning a few calories. Sometimes I thought he burnt more calories in his pursuit on the phone than the cycling. The searching on the phone wouldn't stop till he went to the shower room. However the objective of avoiding eye contact or the need to say a hi or all such uncomfortable situation was avoided with the strategic search tactic on the phone.

I would invite you observe yourself and others around you and notice when such interesting behavior is demonstrated. Hope you have fun with it!

# I Elect Humor

## <u>12 *Saturday* Apr 2014</u>

Election 2014 is turning out to be a great pot boiler, more than any other election in the history of India. No matter how stiff the fight and how serious the situation there is always scope for humor and the build-up to this crucial election is no different. I soak in some of the election time humor.

**AAP –** *Mark Twain* said **never pick a fight with people who buy ink by the barrel**. But looks like that's exactly what AAP has done and their leaders get generously bathed with ink. Ofcourse one might ask, in this digital age when pen is hardly used, leave apart the ink pen, who is buying so much of ink? Also AAP seems to have found the easiest tool to differentiate the good from the bad – A Cap!! Unfortunately AAP supporters have been given only two choices to make, either they could be a Congress B team or they are wrong; no middle path exists.

**BJP** – this is where things get very interesting. At the moment this party seems to have answer for every problem of mankind and that answer interestingly is a four letter word, in fact it's a name. This party is busy finding MS272. No it's not another flight that went off the radar but it is Modi Sarkar with 272 seats. Such is the fervor around this one man that unfortunately either you support him or you are wrong; no middle path that exists today.

**Congress** – No, no don't start laughing just yet. So, this is a party for whom nothing seems to be going right. Even an interview! The whole party is desperately trying to help a certain individual gain maturity and wisdom, possibly with the help of crash courses. They strongly hope that this was 2004 all over again and probably that is what all members have set their calendars too as well and living in a make believe world. Such is the negativity surrounding them that unfortunately either one is a national traitor or a Congress hater; no middle path exists here either.

While politics is considered to be a field of compromises and middle path, looks like this election there are none. Probably people have become objectivist like ***Ayn Rand***. She once said **there are two sides to every issue: one side is right and the other is wrong, but the middle is always evil**

# Facebook Warrior

## <u>20 *Sunday* Apr 2014</u>

The social media, especially Facebook has thrown up many interesting concepts. I explored two interesting phenomenon earlier. First was that of a Facebook Celebrity and the second was that of Facebook Diarrhea. There is one more interesting phenomenon that caught my attention as, I am sure, it would have of many.

In another of my earlier blog I talked about the uniqueness of this social media platform. It hence challenges all conventional ideas of personal and public. If you are on Facebook then you are helpless but to read mundane updates, see selfies, get to know where your friends are, what they are eating and many more of the whims and fancies of your friends or their friends or of people who Facebook thinks you might know or want to know about! This is definitely leading to blurring of the lines between private and public life. What it also does is it gives a platform to instantly express ones opinion about anything under the sky, criticize anyone or appreciate anyone. This freedom is overwhelming and empowering at the same time. Overwhelming because the swelling emotions and pent up feelings have a place to be expressed yet their reach is limited and might not even reach those who it is intended for, yet that people can express and that increasingly organizations or high placed individuals or celebrities are on social media listening to their fans, makes it very empowering too.

What this is leading to, is a phenomenon that I want to call as **Facebook Warrior**. Let me explain. In our day to day lives we see many wrongs happening around us. Whether it is bribe seeking traffic policeman, upstarts driving in the wrong direction in a one way lane, bribes in government offices, indifferent managers, hurting partners, child labor, violence, poor civic sense and many more. There are some very irritating and stubborn social issues as well that refuse to be washed away. We have many who are going out there and under the umbrella of many NGOs or NFOs are working hard and doing their bit in bringing about a change. Yet, there are many who feel strongly about issues such as these but haven't figured out what to do about them. Social Media has resolved this dilemma for them. Now they have the all empowering option – they can tweet! They can post on Facebook!

Mind you this breed of warriors is very prompt. They don't lose anytime in speaking up against what they perceive as a wrong doing. Equipped with smart phones they are the journalist and cameraman rolled into one. Instantaneous videos, on the fly pics and agitated comments are captured and posted on Facebook with amazing alacrity. There are no off days either. These warriors might be lazing on a Sunday afternoon on their couch, but suddenly something they see on the TV agitates them and outcomes the smartphone/tablet/laptop and out goes the fury in the form of words and expressions. The responsible citizens that they are, nothing escapes their acute attention. I have seen some funny instances like, a person who noticed a car not appropriately parked and unnecessarily eating into the adjacent parking space, instead of speaking with the owner of the car, decided to vent out on Facebook with pictures. A person wronged by an Auto driver, instead of reporting it to a nearby police station, waited till he reached home to vent out frustration on Twitter and Facebook. The list goes on.

The posts or tweets are not like articles in the newspaper. They are not dead; they are alive and throbbing with pain and agitation. They attract instant reaction from other warriors online who either agree with the expressed opinion or are completely anti to it. The messages of sympathy and likes and shares they are real victory for a Facebook warrior. The number of likes and messages, obviously, measuring the extent of success. I am sure many among us would identify with the described warrior. Before anybody could even try to raise a finger at me, let me admit, I am one of them!

# Miscellaneous

# The Bong Blast

## <u>26 *Friday* Oct 2012</u>

India is a land of festivals. The various religions that blend into the fabric of the Indian society give innumerable occasions to celebrate with tremendous amount of fanfare and frenzy. Dusshera is one such festival that celebrates victory of the good over the evil and also salutes the power of women. Of all the places it is celebrated in, I would have to say, with certain authority that, no place could compare with the festivities in West Bengal during this occasion and specifically Kolkata than anywhere else.

Dusshera is celebrated by Bengalis world over as Durga Puja. Durga is a Goddess that represents women power and created to take on and defeat the evil in the world. The clay idols of Durga are created each year she and her entourage are kept in a bamboo and cloth based structure created and decorated specifically for this occasion called **Pandals**. All of this is done in localities around Kolkata with contribution from inhabitants of that locality. The scale of the Pujas in Kolkata has grown over period of time and from community contribution based Pujas, it has gone on to attract corporate sponsorship. As time passed and traditions became flexible there were greater experiments brought into the style of conducting Pujas, this gave way to many competitions. Now panel of judges visit all the Pandals and judge which one had a better pandal or a better idol or the general theme and award those localities accordingly. Today Durga Puja is conducted all across the world, especially USA/UK/Germany/Singapore/Malaysia/Melbourne, it also does the work of fostering community feeling as everybody contributes to conduct these Pujas

I won't be wrong if I were to say that, the life of a Bengali pretty much revolves around the Durga Puja. It is a festival that the young and the old of the family equally look forward to with equal enthusiasm. What does it mean to be in Kolkata during this time? I don't know how much could be explained or expressed in words, I guess it is more about a sight to behold and a thing to be experienced. The frenzy or fervor of the occasion is tough to capture in words or even a picture, it is about thousands of localities conducting Durga Pujas, it is about extravagant lighting literally in every nook and corner of the city, it is about oceans and oceans of people till wherever eye could see, it is about one locality trying to outdo the other in its Pandal decoration and theme, it is about street food, it is about long hours of walking going from one locality to the other, it is about time ceasing to exist or have any meaning as night blends into day and day blends into night, it's about passion. This is a time when everything else takes backseat, anything celebrated at such a large scale and with such fervor would obviously have withdrawal syndrome when it all comes to an end as everything does. I present to you some of the choicest pictures from the 2012 Kolkata Durga Puja.

**Beautiful clay idols of Goddess Durga:**

Believe it or not these are all structures made of Bamboo/Cloth/and other recyclable items only for the 4-5 days of the festival:

# Rained Down Senses

## 20 _Wednesday_ Mar 2013

How many times have we appreciated a particular rain sequence from a movie? In certain movies rain forms the essential back drop and also plays a role in intensely depicting the feelings of the protagonist or any character from the movie. Not to forget that rain has also been used as a proxy for a 'head to toe' drenched heroine, that titillates audience' senses and ensures ringing cash registers. I am sure some or most of us have enjoyed and appreciated such rain sequences in movies.

Today, we stay in times that are about scarcity of resources, that are about struggle to be at the right place at the right time to get just about sufficient resources and consider ourselves to be lucky. What were once considered to be abundant and birth right of every human have now become scarce or are available at a premium. Water has become one such resource. Life without water is unimaginable. Foreseeing tremendous stress on availability of potable/drinkable water, various forms of water conservation methodologies have been proposed in the past two decades. Mindless and unplanned expansion of population is only going to put further stress on the available water resources. Such has been the fear over availability of water that China has occupied Tibet to safe guard its water requirements and they say if there ever is a WW III, it is would be to safe guard water requirements.

With such a stress on this resource, almost unnoticed and unquestioned our Movie industry continues to use artificial means to depict rain, flood and drench heroines with water. Have we ever wondered how many liters of water would have literally gone down the drain which could probably have been sufficient to fulfill the water needs of many of our water starving cities? Just sample the extent of water wasted by some of the movies:

Titanic – 60 million Gallons
My Name is Khan – 2,400,000 liters
Tum Mile – 3,600,000 Liters
Dabangg – 180,000 liters
Godzilla – No data
Jurassic Park – No data

Even the much loved movie in Bollywood, 3 idiots had an elaborate rain cum flood sequence, though I was not able to locate exact number of liters used for filming those scenes, but nonetheless, a wastage anyway (Wonder what Aamir Khan has to say about this – Satyamav Jayate?). Imagine, many such movies were made over the years, across world. How much millions of liters or gallons of water that possibly could have been used for more noble purpose, have been wasted just to entertain us!

Can the film industry think of a better way of filming these sequences? Or can the audience stop expecting such rain sequences in movies and choose, sanity over pleasure or titillation?

# Buddy Wiser Inc.

## <u>03 *Wednesday* Apr 2013</u>

Life is a journey into the unknown. Each day unfolds with umpteen possibilities, ofcourse, partly influenced by our actions of yesterday and by our preparatory action in anticipation of the tomorrow. Much like a roller coaster, life cruises ceaselessly with its regular but unpredictable ups and downs. I think the vicissitudes of life become bearable due to the friends that we make during the course of our life. While we live to please our relatives, it is the friends who help us in achieving or doing whatever we set out to do in this life.

Friendship, like many things in life, comes in various forms and is very fluid in nature. It easily acquires the shape of the 'cast' that we desire to keep it in. With time friendship evolves and takes on newer meaning. What makes friendship special is that it is a voluntary act of choosing who one wants to associate with. More often than not we attract people who think alike or have similar goals or share similar views about life. At times we have to talk and exchange views to make friends and yet there are times where non-verbal communication plays a key role in building a subtle friendship. We realize that being born in a particular family is a matter of chance but friends are a matter of choice. Often through course of life we find out that ties of friendship could be stronger and more meaningful than ties of blood.

I think, friendship becomes so strong because friends don't come with any baggage or prior expectations, they accept us as we are today, and there is no incessant need to please each other, or give gifts to each other. In addition it also gives the freedom to criticize with no loss of dignity or fear of insult. There is no stress or pressure on us to maintain or stick onto a friendship for all our life, some friendship ripe. *A summation of me is a summation of all my friends.* Friendship, unlike any other relationship, cuts across barriers of caste, creed, religion, language, nationality or sex. As does friendship come in various forms so does come its expiry date. Some friendships expire with death whereas some friendships expire as the original reason ceases to exist. Nonetheless, it is a voluntary act and I think that is the key factor why we are most comfortable when amongst friends.

I have had the privilege of having some great friends through the course of my life till date. I know for sure that, life wouldn't have been enjoyable or fulfilling or plausible without the presence of the friends who have helped me survive, strive and grow. I am sure I am not isolated in thinking so.

# Wiedergeburt

## <u>25 *Thursday* Jul 2013</u>

Despite all the progress that Humans have collectively made, many fundamental problems of life continue to be a mystery or remain unresolved. On the foundation of such unresolved problems and mysteries stands the structure of human life. The construct seems concrete enough and largely works, till the fundamental questions/problems are revisited. The moment even one such unresolved problem is raised it creates a severe disturbance; opinion and counter-opinion fly from all over. Yet, when hours would have passed one would have realized that they have progressed no further than where they started!

Something did break loose when a friend of mine, during a discussion, brought up the topic of Rebirth/Reincarnation. It is a topic that is old unresolved and unconcluded yet something that we have brushed aside as life continues irrespective of whether we humans understand it or whether we have managed to find an explanation for the confusion or not. As happens in moments of such sudden disruption, my mind started racing and I was breathing heavy, trying to grapple with the matter at hand and think about all the points and counter-points related to it. Needless to say that, the argument was inconclusive and refused to reach anywhere. Especially in times when the line between scientific assumptions and religious beliefs has significantly blurred, finding a consistent and unified explanation proved elusive.

All the major religions of the world, with varying degree and in somewhat ambiguous tone have spoken about re-birth. Most of them tend to speak about rebirth as retribution to the volitional activities that one might have undertaken in previous or the current birth. They also speak about rebirth as multiple attempts by the human soul gets to reach perfection required to put an end to the cycle of birth and rebirth. Ofcourse matters of religion are about belief and often may have nothing do with rational thinking. Though, attempts have been made to rationalize certain beliefs either to convince the fence sitters or to reach out to atheists. Though, I would say, reincarnation is a matter that could baffle and question the rational theories of the staunchest of atheists.

Personally, I think, the question of re-incarnation presents a dilemma. Accepting that there is such a thing appears inconsistent with many of the other beliefs that I hold. Let me present some of the points for which I feel that it is completely inconsistent and incoherent with other beliefs and human endeavor:

- Past life decides the quality of next birth
- Assumes presence of an omniscient and omnipotent force that is monitoring all human activities – automatically takes atheists out of the equation
- Assumes superiority of human birth over and above all other species
- Suggests that the geography, religion, family one is born in is not a matter of chance but a result of previous life
- Sort of indicates graded quality of living where one form of living has got to be superior to the other as a reciprocation of the good behavior of past life or current life
- Completely turns the argument of equality among humans on its head and sort of sides with Hitler

- Completely changes the meaning and context of 'Free Will'
- Mocks the entire effort to fight poverty and injustice
- Appears escapist

Having said that, facts that have come up in recent times makes it tough to refute rebirth. Dr Ian Stevenson, did a study involving about 20 kids who started talking about events of past life pretty much immediately after learning to speak. It is baffling and begs for an acceptable explanation. The only recourse between the two extreme positions could possibly lie in accepting a non-causal reincarnation. However we might still be very far from the possible last word.

Thanks to all the respondents who took the survey and gave us a chance to see what the widespread belief was. Based on the survey I present the summary of the findings that emerged.

- An overwhelming majority of the respondents were Religious
- Though their belief in reincarnation of Religious people was only marginally higher than the non-Religious respondents:
- Over all only 36% of the respondents believed in Reincarnation
- Off the people who believed in Reincarnation – 75% believed our past birth has a strong bearing on our current birth

| | |
|---|---|
| Religious | 72.7 |
| Non-Religious | 27.3 |
| Off Religious people who believed in Reincarnation | 37.5 |
| Off Non-Religious people who believed in Reincarnation | 33.0 |

Survey Results

# Of Debut Retirement and Death

## <u>09 *Thursday* Jan 2014</u>

Years come and years go. Each year leaves an impression on us. We don't essentially come out of any year the same as we entered it. Every year has some significant events that change us and hence the world around us. I recount some of the key events as per me of 2013 – **The Year That Was**.

**Debut:**

It was a case of obituaries being written much before a birth. **Aam Aadmi Party** made a spectacular debut in the world of Indian politics by winning unexpected number of seats in the elections of the State of Delhi. While they are still wet behind the ear when it comes to political discourse or administrative skills, however for a party that was launched just 6 months prior to the elections, for a party that everyone dismissed as an 'also ran', it was a stupendous success. Of course Aam Aadmi Party's victory cannot immediately be called as an 'Aam Aadmi's' (Common Man's) victory, but from being nonexistent to becoming the ruling party in Delhi in 6 months flat is nothing short of a miracle. I hope they succeed through both their success and failure. We need to wait and watch before concluding on this matter.

## Retirement:

Retirement is a very emotional and demanding decision for any individual. To retire from something that one has dedicated one's whole life to and stop doing that something that has given meaning to one's life is not an easy task. Most of our identities are closely entangled with what we do for a living, so retirement could be scary. 2013 saw two emotional farewells of two cricketing stalwarts, two greats of the modern era. While both exited on a high by being part of winning teams but their respective retirements stood out in contrast.

**Sachin Tendulkar** – retired after playing for 24 years for Indian Cricket Team. It was a remarkable career in more ways than one. I don't remember Sachin not playing or not being part of the team for all these 24 years except when injured, even in the worst calendar year as per his standards he still scored more than many of the other top cricketers. There was a media frenzy much ahead of the last match the man would play and everyone associated with the game or otherwise had something to say about it.

**Jacque Kallis** – retired after playing for 18 years for South African Cricket Team. Indeed another remarkable career. The world of cricket has seen many great all-rounders, however as per me none better than Kallis. He was as much a match winning bowler as a match winning batsman. He called it quits on a high. Scored a century and helped his team win in his last match. Has always kept a low profile there wasn't much hype or media frenzy behind his retirement. He silently became the best all-rounder of all times and silently bade farewell to cricket and world just let him be.

## Death:

Katha Upanishad says '**one must understand death in order to understand life**'. I feel life is unfair but death can be nothing but fair. The only certainty that everybody could be certain about in Life is Death. What I wanted to recount here are some of the well-known personalities we lost last year:

Nelson Mandela – a Gandhi or Martin Luther King of our times.

Manna Dey: A singer par excellence

Pran: A unparalleled character actor with a rich baritone. Adapted unique mannerism in each movie to make the characters alive and memorable.

Farooq Sheikh: With Deepti Naval and Sai Paranjpe, Farooq formed a team that gave classics like Katha that are difficult to forget

Margret Thatcher: Capitalism and free markets wouldn't have been what they are today without Thatcher. Thatcher along with Reagon changed the world.

Amar Bose: Man behind BOSE. the company that produces awesome sound systems and equipment

Lalgudi Jayaraman: Carnatic Classical violinist

Shakuntala Devi: Geniuses are always an Enigma. Nonetheless nobody can forget the puzzle books that Shakuntala Devi came out with. At one point of time they were a must for anyone seeking jobs in one of the foremost software company in India.

<u>Mikhail Kalashnikov</u>: Some names get detached from the person and become a property of everyone. Kalashnikov is almost synonymous with machine guns now.

<u>Rituparno Ghosh</u>: A film maker in the moulds or Satyajit Ray. It is good that he didn't have to hear Supreme Court of India declaring illegality of certain sexual preferences.

**If there is a soul and if it is at the mercy of me wishing them peace then, may all their souls rest in peace.**

That sums up what 2013 was all about. 2014 is upon us and as is the case with time it is linear and unidirectional. Good or Bad whatever memories we carry forward from 2013 we can only hope for a great 2014. One thing is certain that 2014 will be just as uncertain as 2013 or 2012 or …

**Happy New Year!!**

# The Other Cast

## <u>16 *Sunday* **Mar 2014**</u>

There are many things in life that become obvious only through their absence. The supporting characters that many actors play in a television series or a movie, literally fighting for both screen space and mind space makes for some interesting observation.

While the hero and heroine have it easy with tailor made roles and dialogs, it is the supporting characters who, I think, have to demonstrate very high level of commitment and dedication to the characters they are playing to make it stand out and linger in our memory. The language of the series or movie doesn't matter. I would like to believe it is the same everywhere and anywhere.

Of seeing Bollywood movies over the years I have started to idolize some these side characters that make watching movies so much a pleasure. Repeat viewing of these movies makes the contribution of these actors stand out even more. I present 4 such contemporary actors who have been a delight to watch in every movie that they have been a part off. Some of them are celebrities in their own rights but probably not as much as the lead actors or actresses of the movies that they are part of.

**Sanjay Mishra** – this guy came into prominence during 1999 world cup as Apple Singh and since then he has lit up many movies with his comic timing. People who haven't seen much of his work, I strongly recommend movies like One Two Three or Dhamaal. His body language, diction, facial expressions and dialog delivery all are a big plus in bringing alive some very ordinary characters. I believe him to be a very underrated actor who might not have entirely got his due. He also blows life into his character in a television series, again that I strongly recommend, Office Office, where despite acting along side a very talented star cast he manages to hold his own.

**Manoj Pahwa** – this guy has been around since the time TV started in India and he acted in the very first hindi soap of Indian television Hum Log. Of course he was much thinner and younger, however both age and growing gait has not depreciated his acting ability or comic timing. He is capable of delivering power packed performances. People unaware of his works, I strongly recommend Aloo Chat, Singh is King, Wanted and also the television series Office Office. Another underrated actor with some amazing performances in every outing.

**Mukesh Tiwari** – this guy made his acting debut in a movie called China Gate in a negative role. He received a lot of praise for his debut performance, however I think he found his true calling in comedy. Every outing in a comic role has been a stupendous performance. Probably doesn't get as much recognition as much as he deserves but I find him amazing in every role he played including the recent performance in Chennai Express as a tamil speaking Sardaar police officer. Some other notable roles were in movies like One Two Three, Gangajal or Arakshan etc.

**Deepak Dobriyal** - probably less talented than the rest that I talk about above, however still capable of showing tremendous commitment to all the roles played by him and making them as much memorable as possible. With a slight built he might have been missed in most of the movies that he has played important parts in. Tanu weds Manu definitely stands out as a great performance as a close friend and confidante of the male protagonist. He was equally good in gripping movies like Omkara or Maqbool

This is a small dedication to the performances of these artistes that I find have special talent of playing the most nondescript roles with great conviction and bring those characters alive to add color and value to the movies that they are part off. I sometimes wonder what their motivation is to keep going at a work that probably doesn't recognize their contribution as much as it should. Of course there have been similar such characters during various generation of Bollywood and even in the current generation there are more who have done an excellent job, however I pick four as per my liking and taste.

# Read not as Written

How often have we seen is that there is a gap between what is written and what is read. Often the state of mind we are in influences how we interpret a written word or phrase. The same holds good for a picture or a symbol. The mind undoubtedly plays a trick in such interpretations.

Let me give two examples:

Same way a written word is, more often than not, not interpreted the same way as it is meant to. The mind plays tricks and influences what we finally interpret from what we see and read. The interpretation that I speak of, is not only about know the meaning of the used word but goes beyond it and is more about the drawn perception upon reading the word. Another example is:

**Aoccdrnig to rscheearch at Cmabrigde Uinervtisy, it deosn't mttaer in waht oredr the ltteers in a wrod are, the olny iprmoetnt tihng is taht the frist and lsat ltteer be at**

**the rghit pclae. The rset can be a total mses and you can sitll raed it wouthit a porbelm. Tihs is bcuseae the huamn mnid deos not raed ervey lteter by istlef, but the wrod as a wlohe. Amzanig, huh?**

You can't read what is written but can perceive what it is meant to convey! Amazing mind at work again! Of course the examples I presented above had deliberate and obvious distortions with an objective of demonstrating that our interpretation/perception is what carries the maximum weightage than what is actually written.

In our day to day life, sentences or words with no obvious distortions or hidden tricks can still lead to different interpretation/perception by different individuals and hence influence their following reactions, and it doesn't even have to be those phrases that carry different things in different cultural context. Each written word becomes a stimulus, stimulating different responses based on an individual's perception. Sometimes the brain doesn't even wait till the entire phrase, sentence or paragraph is completely read. Even if completely read, still certain keywords could trigger a perception completely different than what is written. So, often we see debates digressing from the problem statement and snowball in a different direction till, someone intervenes, re-states the problem statement and bring the focus of the debate back to the agenda at hand.

Memory has a role to play in the building of perception. One needs to pay attention to what one is feeding into the brain and committing to memory. Once committed it plays a powerful role in influencing what we perceive from a written word. Next time when anyone decides to react upon a written word, we must ensure we read and re-read what is written and not react based purely on our perception.

Reality is how we interpret it. Imagination and volition play a part in that interpretation. Which means that all reality is to some extent a fiction.

**-Yann Martel**

# Clubs and Witch

Recently there was a big ruckus created about a judge not being allowed into a club in Chennai (India) as he turned up in unacceptable attire. The unacceptable attire happened to be traditional South Indian dress. The media and people went into frenzy, criticizing the club saying such imposed dress codes are discriminatory and a result of colonial hangover. So much so that the State Government had to issue a threat of cancelling the club's license, echoing the public outcry. I personally though, have a different take on this matter.

I think discrimination is a strong word and needs to be used carefully. Only and only when one is denied any of the fundamental rights due to some misplaced reason, can discrimination be said to have been done for example, human dignity. Every human being has a right to dignity and if he is denied that then he is definitely being discriminated against. In this context a club membership is neither mandatory nor a fundamental human right, so whatever the club decides to do definitely can't be called as discrimination. Also there is no news of the club having denied membership on the basis of caste, creed, color or nationality.

That having said, it only leaves out the point of dress. The only real question to be asked is, whether the club makes it clear any dress code to be followed in its terms and conditions while offering membership. As long as it does, it has the right to deny entry to anyone who has agreed to follow the code of conduct but doesn't adhere to it. Such denials definitely don't tantamount to discrimination. If we question the club about its right to impose a dress code, then we need to question Schools, Colleges, Armed Forces and any other such private or public enterprises that impose similar dress codes. Also not to forget that an individual has the choice of refraining from taking membership of any such club which doesn't accept the attire he/she is most comfortable in.

I believe that Government stepping in and enacting a law that would prevent such Clubs from denying entry to people in unacceptable attires is not the right. Infact Government should have never stepped in, it sets a wrong precedence. The matter must have been left to the club and its members to decide and sort out.

I would also like to infact applaud the Club. At least it didn't discriminate or show special privileges and had the guts to stop a High Court judge when found at fault! That's rare in this country.

# Pacem in Terris

## <u>23 *Saturday* Aug 2014</u>

Man is in perennial pursuit of peace, a self-sustaining, self-fulfilling and self-deluding pursuit. Everything that man does is done in the pursuit of peace. God's are for peace, Religions are for peace, Countries are for peace, Economic progress is for peace, Weapons are for peace and even wars are for peace, yet peace has eluded mankind till date. There is very little to show for all the efforts spent in this pursuit of peace, there is conflict somewhere or the other.

It intrigues me, why despite centuries of pursuit we have not had any success in achieving peace. I think the answer lies in how we view peace. We view peace as a 'goal' that we want to achieve. The problem with this view point is that it automatically includes a subjective interpretation of what peace means. The problem with subjective interpretation is the co-existence of multiple, incoherent and antithetical interpretations that automatically mean conflict. Hence I say the pursuit of peace is self-delusional, as hidden behind is an inadvertent rise of conflict.

I think that 'peace' can never be a goal. Nobody can pursue peace or achieve peace. Only when all pursuits of man have ended that peace is what would remain. As long as we are in pursuit of something or the other, including peace, we will only know one or the other form of conflict but never peace. Yes a subjective interpretation of peace or something that looks like peace might exist but not PEACE. I think J Krishnamurti was right when he said *Peace can only exist if we have complete security, both outwardly and inwardly, psychologically and environmentally*

# Academic Proportions

## 22 *Monday* Sep 2014

There is a term called **Academic Inflation**. By this I don't mean the increasing cost of education. What I mean by it is a situation where jobs which needed lesser qualifications are now able to attract applicants with higher qualification. I find this phenomenon very intriguing and certainly worth some exploration. The obvious explanation, that many would offer is that of increasing population. Certainly population is a factor especially because the Academic Inflation seems to be more of a developing economy' phenomenon, however I strongly believe the reason is much more serious than just increasing population.

I think the reason lies in pursuing a course or a curriculum that is in demand and dictated by market requirement and not pursuing a course or curriculum as per one's aptitude. In the blind rush to be among the people who could take advantage of existing trends in job market people take up courses that they often don't have much aptitude for. In this process firstly there are more number of people with the same qualification but a very small number of people with the required aptitude and hence majority find it tough to get through job interviews. Frustrated with the situation many turn towards additional certifications, diplomas or second degrees, then reapply for jobs they could have got with their first degree. Also, even after getting the job most of the people would definitely find it tough to get noticed ahead of the people who have a natural aptitude towards the subject and job. In this I am not even touching the abstract topic of job satisfaction to make my point.

It is also because of this blind rush to line up for courses that are in demand that people indirectly encourage institutions to increase their cut-offs and also fees. Also if one institution becomes more popular and renowned for getting cushy jobs for its students, then one can imagine how the demand and supply would play out. So, not only is one paying more for the same degree, one probably is also gaining more degrees than is required for the job they want to apply for. At present the academic inflation is caught in a perennial vicious cycle. This is certainly a problem created both by the societal pressure and Government policies. Though I think the role played by parents and friends is of prime importance.

Can academic inflation be reversed or contained? I think it certainly can be. To start with parents need to encourage kids to find things that they like doing or enjoy doing. Parents must also observe the natural aptitude demonstrated by kids to see what comes easy and with less enforcement. Based on such observations the subjects to be taken up and hence the career to be chosen could become clear. More than the getting of the job the encouragement has to be to master the subjects one is interested in by not only focusing on marks but also the practical application in outside world. Once mastery is achieved on subjects the rest usually tends to fall in place as far as jobs are concerned. Genuine interest in subjects leads to additional drive to learn, it develops a passion which often is the essential ingredient to succeed in any endeavor. Any additional qualification or second degree sought would be to either enhance one's knowledge or have access to resources which one degree can't genuinely put them in touch with. Such second degrees don't cause academic inflation but genuinely create intellectual capital which in turn has the power to fuel innovation and many industry implementable ideas.

Being run of the mill and falling in a rat race and running in a direction that majority are running is certainly not the right way to start. Self-realization followed by pursuit of excellence and a non-stop desire to be the best that one could be in the chosen field is the only way to avoid academic inflation

# Philosophy

# Consciousness – My Journey I

No topic evokes greater passion or draws out greater debate than a discussion on Consciousness. It is something that we all possess and we think we know what it could possibly be. While for any other matter related to the body people are ready to talk to a specialist and one might even not hesitate visiting a Psychologist or a Psycho-therapist yet, about Consciousness we think we know it, we don't need to consult any specialist on it. Even if a specialist is to be consulted it would be someone in the realm of spiritual or religious domain. I think, lot of people might say that, consult, is a heavy word for such a meeting; 'seeking guidance' is where one would like to put it. This is the thing about Consciousness; everybody knows something but may be, nobody knows everything about it.

This subject of consciousness has moved out of the realm of Spirituality, Religion and Philosophy and also entered an Objective field like Science, lot of scientific experiments, especially after the advent of Quantum Mechanics/Physics, have become difficult to comprehend without factoring Consciousness into it. This as a subject can engulf all other subjects. Some may point out that, if we don't understand this then we might not understand anything else and yet there may be some who would say this is tough to understand let us leave this aside and understand other things independent of it.

In usual parlance we associate a lot of mysticism with Consciousness, the modern day effort however is to associate lot of realism to it and reduce the element of mysticism. So, when we talk of consciousness one would always be keen to know what form of Consciousness are we talking about? Restricting ourselves to Human Consciousness, might be a good way to start an scientific experiment, however if the idea is to understand Consciousness then we have to understand all other types along with Human Consciousness. The following are the types of Consciousness that I realise we might need to focus on

- Human Consciousness
  o Sub-Conscious
  o Unconscious
  o Meta Conscious
  o Sleep
  o Coma
  o Death
  o Anesthesia
  o Local
  o Non-Local
  o Sensual
  o Non-sensual
- Animal Consciousness [Most of the above sub-factors apply]
- Plant Consciousness [Most of the above sub-factors apply]
- Consciousness of Non-Living matter
- Consciousness in Nature
- Consciousness of an atomic/sub-atomic particle
- Consciousness in the Universe

There could be many many more forms that we could think of and could add to this list. Each of these topics have now become areas of big scientific experiments and also equally occupy hallowed place in the field of Philosophy. As history would suggest, Philosophical understanding has always fueled Scientific development and discoveries. So we can only hope that both these fields feed of each other and give us a greater understanding of this subject than what exists today and make it available for public consumption.

Let me start my journey into this by asking some basic questions

- Does Consciousness Exist?
- Where does it reside?
- What is Consciousness?
  o Nature of Consciousness
  o Is it Matter of Energy
- Can Consciousness be studied
  o Will understanding Consciousness solve some of the long standing problems of science?

**Does Consciousness Exist?**

A Human being, as I see it, is a combination of an Objective aspect and an Subjective aspect. Objective are the ones that all of us can see and qualify ex: the body, hair, eyes etc. subjective is the unique point of view, internal interpretation to events, personal experience (Qualia) that the person brings with him which is not tangible but nonetheless observable.

This subjective aspect is what people commonly call as Consciousness (CS) in one of it's form, so I could say yes it does exist, however we don't know where is it emerging or originating from. Yet there are other important questions that come up, like

- What happens to my consciousness when I fall asleep?
- When I dream in my sleep is that another type of consciousness?

There is a strong nature of subjectivity associated with it that makes coming at any mutually agreed consensual understanding, extremely tough. The moment I think I have a grasp of it, it suddenly opens up into plethora of options leaving me exactly where I started. Today Neuroscience has made significant progress in mapping the brain and also understanding the functioning of each aspect, and the areas of the brain responsible for feelings like anger, happiness, anxiety have been determined. So much so that as far as human consciousness is concerned we have something called Neural Co-relate of Consciousness (NCR) which attempts to explain everything about Consciousness by understanding the neural functions. Yet one can't be certain that after all the functioning of a brain in a certain individuals body is completely understood and if it was to be transplanted into another individual's body whether it would still have similar functionality. I am guessing that study of mono-zygotic or identical twins could possibly make an interesting read.

How about CS in animals? Knowing that animals also possess feelings like humans and interpret and act to situations it would be safe to assume that they do possess some form of CS even if not entirely similar to Human CS.

While above aspect needs further arbitration, what is even more interesting to find out is do Plants possess CS or does non-living matter possess CS? Jagadish Chandra Bose had demonstrated that Plants also react to stimuli, similar to humans, and if spoken to Plants are capable of reacting. It is also well known that they sure possess intelligence to make the roots grow in the direction of water and the shoots in the direction of sunlight. Also it's proven that a tree can be drugged or put under influence of anesthesia before being transplanted at a different location. So all indications that even if not exactly similar to Human or Animal CS Plants also possess some form of CS.

Even more interesting aspect to dwell on is, does non-living matter possess CS? I was, at the very outset, instinctively, wanted to dismiss this notion all together. However the more I thought the more it became blurry and I could not distinguish Non-Living / Living and definitely about CS.

It is well known that Life took form in the aquatic world and from non-living elements that under some special condition and situation gave rise to a living form. If a living form has an origin in non-living then, non-living matter should also possess some elements of CS. Most Spiritual practices suggest knowing and becoming one with CS is the ultimate aim of human life. Yet as per widely accepted theory everything started from the Big Bang. If knowing CS is the ultimate aim then CS should have existed even before Big Bang and been the cause for the big bang. In that case living or non-living become just different manifestation of CS. There are many more thoughts like these that can blur the lines between living/non-living and what can or cannot possess CS.

A subject like Consciousness is not something that I could have thought of covering in a single publication on this blog. I shared an aspect of the journey taken by me to understand CS and see what different approaches people have adopted and if we could come to a universal agreement by approaching the same subject from various fields. I will continue sharing my journey as we go along.

# Consciousness – My Journey II

## <u>02 *Tuesday* Oct 2012</u>

**What is Consciousness?**

As discussed in the last post on the same topic, a definite answer to the question is tough to reach. Most scientists today agree that CS has two essential dimensions to it:

- Arousal [Level of Consciousness]

General belief is that we are Conscious when we are awake and lose Consciousness when we fall asleep. Through the facts I present here, I would like to argue by presenting various facts that Sleep is a form of Consciousness. Every other form of unconscious existence, we know off is also a subset of consciousness. Let me present the facts and try and explain myself.

- Awareness [Content of Consciousness]

We have intentional awareness of what we decide to pay attention to as well as have unintentional awareness. The bodily operation play a key role in deciding on this content with inputs from sense organs, though here I would like to argue that experiences or perception of what we sense largely depends on the memories we form.

Let me present the facts and my arguments for perusal.

It has been observed that for **AROUSAL** two aspects of the brain are essential, '**Ascending Reticular Activating System'** **(ARAS)** and the '**Cerebral Cortex'**. These are the parts of the brain that are essential for us to wake up every morning and are shutdown when we fall asleep. There is tremendous amount of research that has been done to understand ARAS and CC, so that cures to various sleep disorders may be found. Damage to ARAS or Cerebral cortex or the areas around it, could lead one into a state of partial wakefulness but complete unawareness either of oneself or the environment (**Persistent Vegetative State or PVS**). It could also lead to a state of being unawake and unaware (**Coma**). Sleep/Coma is popularly believed to be loss of CS brought about by the shutdown of ARAS and Cerebral Cortex (CC). However our personal experience would indicate that even when we are asleep, an alarm or someone calling our name could arouse us (factors that can arouse us vary from person to person). Also there are many instances where people have woken up from Coma (albeit with some mental disorders) indicating that the Consciousness is still present, awaiting the right trigger to wake up.

This means that sleep or Coma is not a complete loss of Consciousness; a form of CS does exist, and ARAS and CC are not shutdown but remain in standby or hibernation awaiting a stimulus to wake them up. With progress in resolution of pictures developed using **fMRI, EEG or PET**, one can study the brain signals under various conditions and situations. Research done to monitor the brain signals during sleep using these techniques, indicate that during sleep the inputs from Sense organs are active but are attenuated, allowing ARAS and CC to go to standby and not stay in a constant state of arousal. Also ARAS tends to prioritize the attenuated signals from each sense organ to decide the 'urgency of the need' to come out of standby and arouse the person from sleep. (This could indicate an important postulate that **Consciousness is omniscient**). Thus sleep could be seen as a state of partial wakefulness, partial awareness, or a form of unconscious awareness. Similar research is being carried out to understand Coma and the possibilities of reversing it, and also to deal with mental disorders of the person who wakes up from Coma.

While we may not understand unconsciousness awareness, or what is sometimes called subconscious awareness, it hasn't stopped people from claiming that things said, done or thought during unconscious awareness can strongly influence the behavior of a person when fully conscious and fully aware. A separate field has developed to work on unconscious learning vs. conscious learning and has fueled the whole Self Help Group/Books industry to thrive on whatever minimal understanding we have of this state. However what seems to be coming through is that Unconscious is a subset of CS and not mutually exclusive as was believed it to be earlier. Here it is interesting to note that General Anesthesia (though not much is known about how it works) is a way of temporarily shutting down the ARAS and CC so that person stays in a state of "un-awakened unawareness" and hence feels neither the pain nor has any memory of the performed operation, and wakes up when the effect of anesthesia wears off. This area needs to be researched more to understand the level of Consciousness and the related brain activity. It could also help find ways of reviving a person from Coma or PVS.

The second dimension to Consciousness is **AWARENESS** or the content of Consciousness. What is it that we are aware of? Surroundings? Thoughts? Memories? Sensory inputs? Probably a picture could help us better understand what the bodily functions are and how that leads to the content of Awareness.

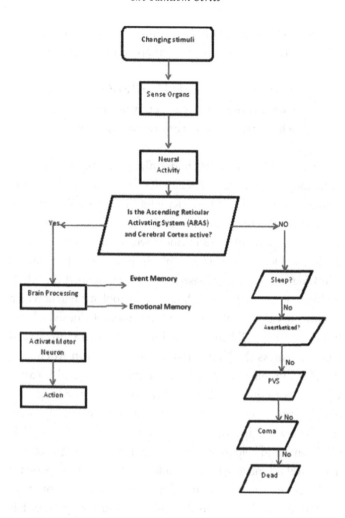

The stimuli mentioned in Fig 1 indicates that it should be "Changing Stimuli"; we slowly lose awareness of any stimuli that don't change. For example if we continue to stare at one point continuously it vanishes, or if we put our feet in hot water after the initial reaction we are unaware of the feel of water on our feet unless the temperature of the water changes.

Very strong philosophical and epistemological question come up. In the above mechanical operation of the body,

- **where is the sense of "I" or "EGO" coming from?**
- **where is the experience coming from?**
- **where are the thoughts emerging from?**

The bodily operation are definitely leading to formation of memory which I feel plays an active role in the content of consciousness and what we actually are aware of. However apart from the memories the body function generates there are other aspects of consciousness which need to be studied in detail. Details of this was nicely put forward by **David Chalmers**. In a paper released in 1995, he divided the whole problem of the content of CS into two problems one of which he chose to call Easy Problem and the other (obviously) a Hard Problem. Easy problem is related to the **Neural Co-relate of Consciousness** (NCC popularised by **Christoph Koch**) and the Hard Problem is what is of the **experience** and is called **Qualia**. For example when I see the color red, the frequency of light wave is converted to signals inside my neural system and the brain helps me to recognize it as a Red color (fMRI/ CT Scan could help to observe the neural processing); yet how does it feel for me to see the red color, and what that experience is like is the Qualia. As per Chalmers, Qualia is tough to understand, and it is also difficult to figure out where it is coming from? Here I would like to highlight the role played by **memory**.

Memory possibly plays a key role in the experience that we have in a particular situation. I think it is essential that we understand what memory is and what type of memory gets formed under various conditions as (Ref Fig 2), that in a way influences the real content of Consciousness and hence our perception of what we view, and is probably also responsible for Qualia. The following diagram indicates the formation of memories in a wakeful state.

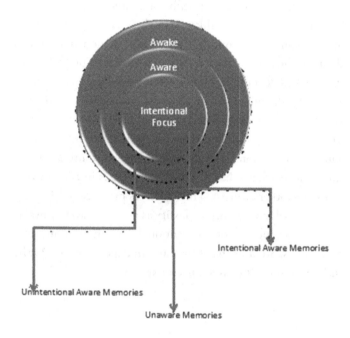

Fig 2

Another area that we don't know much about is about **Consciousness and Intention** and it leads to unresolved philosophical and epistemological questions:.

**Where does the Intention come from?**
**What dictates what a person's intention would be?**

Similarly as seen in Fig 2, we have an unawake but aware state where there are possibilities of formation of memories which strongly influence our perception when awake and aware. At the moment it is not clear if there is any function of Intention in such a state.

Most of what I have said above, has been subject of scientific research and philosophical deliberation and it applies to both Humans and Animals alike. Also there is a high possibility that we cannot rule out that plants also demonstrate similar elements however they are not scientifically proved to an extent where it could be mentioned. I would leave you with an interesting thought and Consciousness among the non-living – 'Anybody with minimal knowledge of Chemistry knows that when we mix two elements there is a predictable and repeatable outcome or reaction. This indicates that at an atomic level each atom knows what it has to do when it comes in contact with atom of another element. This indicates presence of Memory; a memory which we cannot classify as aware, unaware, awake, unawake, intentional or unintentional, but a form of memory nonetheless. **So does the atom have an experience or Qualia and hence does it have Consciousness?**

# Matter of Consciousness

## <u>04</u> *<u>Tuesday</u>* <u>**Dec 2012**</u>

CS has been approached in as methodical a manner as possible in my last two blog posts, about the same subject, I also have tried to take a much more structured approach and use my own CS to understand CS itself. Approaches like these, while attempting to get an objective view of a seemingly subjective topic, leave many philosophical conundrums unanswered. I explore one such conundrum here.

In general, all of us do think we fairly understand how the world functions, also based on what our belief systems are, we do also believe that we understand how world would have evolved. In many ways, topics taught in schools and colleges, are taught as definite and well established facts. Such incidents definitely have the power to strongly influence our views and thinking on various matter and almost certainly stop us from questioning some of these assumptions that are passed off as facts. Ofcourse, as long as not closely viewed, the assumptions definitely seem to work just as fine hence we also do not scratch deeper than the surface. Review the two scenarios

**Scenario 1:**

Without thoughts, there is no content of CS
Without memory there are no thoughts
Without time there is no memory

**Implies** -Without time there is no *'content of consciousness'*, what is left is only the *"level of Consciousness"*.

Implies that level of Consciousness is timeless and should have been even present before Big Bang created the universe

Implies matter emerged from CS

**Scenario 2:**

Life emerged from non-living matter long ago

When non-living matter combined in a particular manner and under particular circumstances life was created.

Only if there is life is there a question of Level or Content of CS

**Implies** CS emerges from matter

*CS from Matter or Matter from CS!*

**This probably is the biggest conundrum that there could be.**

# Immemorialis

## <u>18 *Friday* Jan 2013</u>

I boarded the waiting cab and was contentedly on my way to the airport. I wouldn't have gone any further than a Km when, unable to remember something, I broke out into cold sweat. I just couldn't remember whether I had locked the main door of my apartment. I could recollect having closed windows, turning of the gas stove but, darn me, I just couldn't recollect if I had locked the main door. I had to call the security guard to quickly run upstairs to my apartment and check if the door was indeed locked or not!

I was to travel to a nearby city. Just few days before the trip, while buying a consumer electronic item I got a silver coin as part of a promotional offer and kept the coin in my wallet (no good reason why). I thought it would be better if I left the coin at home and went on my trip. I removed the coin from my wallet and left it on my **work table at home**. It was a one night stay at the city that I was visiting. Before I fell asleep in my hotel room that night, for some reason, I thought to myself 'I have left the silver coin on my **hotel room table** and I need to ensure I keep it back into my wallet next day morning before I check out'! Needless to say I broke out into cold sweat next day morning as I could not find the silver coin on the **table at the hotel**!

My friend had finished buying some gifts for friends and relatives. There were no surprises in the bill; however when it came to punching in the PIN for payment by debit card, my friend couldn't remember the PIN at all. He failed repeatedly as he attempted to recollect what it was. I had to divert his attention and then ask him to just punch in the number pad without thinking. Lo! He got the right PIN punched in

The obvious reaction to the above is 'you are growing old' or 'birds of same feather flock together'. Undeniably these observations are true, but not the only truths that exist. Once things like these are stated people tend to come up with innovative advises like, reduce alcohol consumption or even, get married! Needless to say that some advises I have headed to and some I have not. However, it is interesting to delve into this matter, atleast to figure out if I am the odd one out or if I am in bad company.

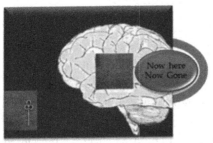

Unsettled and disturbed, I did some empirical research by sending questionnaires to a few of my friends. The questionnaire asked them about situations such as the ones mentioned above and asked if they had faced any or all of them. 100% of the respondents indicated they had definitely experienced atleast one of the mentioned situations and more than 70% indicated they had experienced more than one of them. About 40% said they had experienced all of those. I chose people of various age groups and backgrounds to ensure we are not talking about senility or mental disturbance. After seeing the response, needless to say, I did heave a sigh of relief!

These incidents, seemingly, happen often to us in our day to day lives. They also form the core of researching consciousness. As discussed in an earlier blog, memory is the key factor in deciding the contents of Consciousness. I think in each of the incidents mentioned at the beginning of this post, the memory seems to have transitioned from being an intentional aware memory to being an unaware memory. This I think is synonymous with muscle memory. In other words, the **brain outsources the memory** that doesn't need any processing to the muscles. Hence often when we want to intentionally and with full awareness want to remember certain things that we do routinely, we fail to perform those acts. A car driver or a player of a musical instrument would know what I am talking about. *In each of the above incidents the muscle memory was sufficient to carry out the required activity and needed no active processing by the brain, however when the memory was attempted to be recalled with full awareness of the brain, it couldn't retrieve the unaware memory at all!*

# Uppity Identity

Identities, in a life time we juggle with multiple identities. We are actually a sum total of what our identities make us. All of us have a priority list of identities that we adorn depending upon the situation and circumstances. It is the same order in which these identities have the capacity to make us feel good or hurt us depending upon how other's respond to them.

Nationality, race, ethnicity, religion, football club we love, cricket team we love, baseball team we swear our allegiance with, education we have had, institutions we have attended, profession, political ideology that we agree with, economic ideology we subscribe etc. are all various identities that make us. We are not born with all, definitely they don't matter to us when we die yet, during a lifetime these identities are us and we are our identities. ***Identities are fragile malleable, ductile and continuously divisible***. Hence identities are the source of both internal (within us) and external (in society) conflicts.

The multiple identities that we adorn appear harmless; however a study of human history indicates that all major conflicts have always been conflict of identities. ***Identities need constant nurturing, constant appreciation, and constant acknowledgment***. At any point if an identity is ignored, disrespected, devalued or threatened, then one tends to become extremely protective and sensitive about it and does whatever is needed to prove the relevance, value, superiority of it. Yes, under duress, some identities do tend to become dormant but, there is no indication of any identity ever becoming extinct.

**Second world war** witnessed how Hitler, who gave priority to the Aryan identity of his, went berserk to prove purity and superiority of this identity over the so called defiled identity of Jews and the results of such an effort is now etched in history for us to read and reflect upon.

**Cold War** was a conflict of ideological identities, capitalist trying to prove their superiority and relevance over communist. Again undoubtedly clash of identities, repercussions were quite drastic and it polarized people.

**9/11** incident indicates how an identity that feels threatened, disrespected and condescended upon, reacts, despite loss of civilian lives involved and severe repercussion on how the world would perceive both the identities involved in this conflict.

And we can go on and on, from large scale wars to the riots that break out in football stadiums, all bear testimony to how identities have the power to dictate action. This also means that as an individual if we keep removing and travel backwards in order of importance from one identity to the other we probably might know who we really are and how many of our identities really deserve the importance we give them. On the other hand as a society we understand that if peace is a real and essential objective then one has to appreciate and accept all the multiple identities that exist without paranoia, propaganda or parochialism. Nobel laureate economist Amartya Sen in his essay 'Identity and Violence' says *'**Perbaps the worst impairment comes from the neglect—and denial—of the roles of reasoning and choice, which follow from the recognition of our plural identities. The illusion of unique identity is much more divisive*** *than the universe of plural and diverse classifications that characterize the world in which we actually live. The descriptive weakness of choiceless singularity has the effect of momentously impoverishing the power and reach of our social and political reasoning. The illusion of destiny exacts a remarkably heavy price'*

# Time Series

What is time? Does Time move? I find it very strange when some very innocuous question, about a simple day to day phenomenon, stumps me when asked about. I can't seem to fathom how what I was so sure about, a moment ago, gets decimated into a maze of confusion immediately after being asked to define. Time is one such phenomenon, which has engulfed many leading brains, both ancient and contemporary, in the quest of being understood and explained. Something that is so obvious and seemingly straightforward has been an unresolved mystery for ages.

All the definitions of Time, suffer from circularity. Oxford Dictionary defines time as ***the indefinite continued progress of existence and events in the past, present, and future regarded as a whole: travel through space and time.*** *Similarly there are definitions which state –* **'Time is what prevents everything from happening at once'** *or* **'Time is what can be measured by clocks'. Is time a thing in which all other events happen? Or is time a result of all the events that happen?** There are many fields that incorporate a concept of time but without being able to define it in precise terms, e.g.: Religion, Science, Philosophy etc. Yet we believe our life is a race against time and that time is running out. So another tricky question gets added, does time move? Even a casual observation would reveal that Time is unidirectional and only flows forward; never backward. Ofcourse, in colloquial usage we all would have used phrases like "time stopped for a moment" or "it seemed like ages" or "in a twinkling". Statements like these give another interesting dimension to time that of -our experience!

Philosophers have found themselves divided on the question of "is there existence of time independent of our experience?" That is, is there a clock somewhere that is constantly ticking irrespective of whether I see it or feel it? Some believe in such a concept of Time that is ticking independent of our experience and such a concept has been called *Newtonian Time*. The anti-thesis to this is that time is completely experiential and has no independent existence. A view popularized by Leibniz and Kant.

Interestingly, inspite of all the confusion that exists about Time, we continue to conveniently incorporate it in our lives, run our respective races and carry on without any semblance of doubt. However one thing we are certain as an individual is that, Time seems to end with death. ***Death – what is death? Why do people die? Does the Body have a mechanism to measure the progress of time? Body is formed up of multiple cells; does each cell have a sense of time? If each cell has a lifecycle of its own, then obviously it must have some measure of the progress of time.*** However, if we take humanity as a whole or the world as a whole, death ceases to be the end of time. If we take the entire universe into consideration, time appears to be this phenomenon that's constantly expanding.

At this point, let me introduce another interesting point by defining time as *the gap between two events*. With this definition what happens is that we eliminate the possibility of a beginning of time or an ending of time. If there has to be a concept of time, there have to be two events, for a particular point to be called as beginning of time a prior event should have occurred thus defeating the concept of calling a point as beginning of time. Similarly there cannot be an end of time. Thus, through this logic time neither has a start nor an end. All the religions in the world today have a concept of time. Islam and Christianity believe in linearity of time. In a linear concept of time, applying the aforesaid logic there cannot be a beginning or end of time. So either this means time always existent or that time never existed. Interestingly Hinduism believes in cyclical nature of time. So the beginning becomes the end and the end becomes the beginning. *Time does appear to move. There is the past, the present and the anticipated future. If we take the premise that time doesn't exist then how do we justify the motion of time?*

*Time and the movement of time do appear to be entirely experiential.* However, undeniably, all living organisms age and die. Infact, innumerable cells in the living organism go through their own respective lifecycles and perish. Some of them have lifecycles that are consistent and repeatable, almost as if they were encoded with the factor of time. These cells and cells responsible for aging of all species of the living world are sort of dictated by the memory of this code. A living organism at a macro level also appears to be strongly influenced by memory which in-turn has a strong impact on time and our perception of time. If each of the cell and somehow we, were to lose memory, would we stop aging? Would the body become immortal? On a different plane, if I didn't know how I was and how I looked 5 years ago, I wouldn't know if I have aged even if I look myself hard in the mirror or feel any pain in my body. Experientially I continue to be ageless. If experientially one becomes ageless can one defy death? Interestingly, nothing in our view has escaped the eventuality of death. Among all the uncertainty of life is a certainty and that is about Death. Memory has multiple functions to fulfill. The aspect of memory I am interested in, is the aspect which determines our personality and gives a consistency and continuity to it. It is a recording of all our likes, dislikes, knowledge, aptitude and everything that gives a continuity to our identity and hence our personality. ***The moment I lose this memory, my ego vanishes and so does my experience about time and its movement. I don't know what it would feel like being so, or whether it would feel anything at all [extra sensory], however the external (body) might die yet internally or experientially that death might not mean anything***

# A Play by the Line

We see ego different than us. We treat ego as something that needs to be controlled and restrained. What we fail to realize is that 'We are our Ego'. Everything that we identify ourselves with, name, family, education, body, looks, car we drive, job we do everything becomes part of our Ego and everything becomes part of us. Ego, though, is always built on our past. We believe what we are today is because of all that we have done in the past; not realizing that past doesn't exist. It only lingers in our memory and sticks to us as ego. If we are our ego and ego is us then we are not living in the present but are a mere shadow of our past.

Apart from past we also tend to heavily rely upon our future. The promise of the future is very lucrative and enticing. We believe that whatever we are not today we will become tomorrow. Undoubtedly it is an act of ego to remain dissatisfied with the present and remain in a never ending quest of 'becoming' not realizing that future doesn't exist either.

If we disassociate from the past and thus from our ego and also kill the future, what remains of us? Whatever remains of us will we be able to accept it? No baggage of the past and no anticipation for the future! Does this thought scare us? What would that state be like? Ego is perennially thirsty for more and we are perennially hopeful of our future – if both come to an end – do we become more alive or do we become dead? Do we really ever accept the current moment? Or are we busy sizing up the entire time-line?

# Just Is Complicated

Are we humans born evil? Are we born with an incessant need to commit crime? Are we all born criminals and reformed by society? If we are born as criminals then committing crime is but a natural outcome then why do we punish those few who do end up committing crime? Even if punishment is justified who has the right to punish? Can a group of born criminals be entrusted to punish somebody? Can somebody who commits an act following his natural self, be punished? A bunch of born criminals entrusted with power through some suspicious means punishing an individual for committing an act following his natural self, be called justice?

One might question the reason behind my assumption of 'humans born evil'. I can only point towards our Society's belief in legislated laws to maintain law and order in our day to day life indicates all humans are born criminals waiting for the first chance to commit crime unless reined in by laws. Hence often there is demand for stricter laws and stronger implementation of the same.

The very idea of punishment is an interesting phenomenon as well. Leading thinkers of all ages have questioned justification of punishment and also about who has the moral right to punish? Also how to decide what is an appropriate punishment? When a person is wronged by another person, any attempts by the wronged person to inflict a similar pain on the perpetrator is considered undesirable, unjust and a symbol of uncivilized society. However, after a fair debate and arbitration, if a similar pain is inflicted by the judicial system, it is considered legal, just and mark of a civilized society. Even any attempt by a wrong doer to punish himself is also considered illegal. Thus Justice is a complicated affair without even having to discuss about Capital punishment!!

A whole system cracking down on an individual at times appears to be crueler and unjustified an act than an individual seeking revenge against another. A wronged individual can seek revenge albeit, after a judicial system approves of it and also takes the responsibility of carrying out the agreed revenge. The popular 20th century philosopher **Friedrich Nietzsche**supported this form of punishment and meting justice, he said '***Justice and the institution of law essentially take revenge out of the hands of the offended party. If I am robbed, it is justice, and not myself, that has been harmed, and so justice must claim revenge. Thus, Nietzsche suggests, the concept of justice can only exist in a society that has established laws that can be transgressed: there is no such thing as "justice in itself."***

In the wake of the news of the suicide committed by one of the main accused in the, now popular, Delhi rape case Dec 2012, I would like to inspire people to reflect upon our human behavior, society and the concept of justice.

# Just is as Complicated

A friend of mine tore into me for my assumption of 'we are born evil'. Hence I make an attempt here to understand justice this time assuming we are all born 'as good'.

So say, we are all born as good, yet there are crimes in society, how would one explain crimes in a society where all are born as good? I guess two possible explanations could be offered

- Circumstances force people to commit acts that are undesirable or what is said to be crime
- Circumstances present choices to an individual between the right thing to do and the wrong thing to do
  - o We are all born good so we should always choose the right thing
  - o Some of us are not entirely good and might choose the wrong thing
- Hence acts in society that could be called as crime

If, circumstances are what push a good person to choose the so called wrong thing shouldn't the society collectively take the responsibility of creating such circumstances? Is it appropriate to punish someone who is just a victim of circumstances that were created by the society? Can that be called Justice? If he was born with a genetic disposition to choose the wrong thing, should he be punished for choosing the wrong thing or be treated for it like any one else is for other genetic ailments?

In society we often demand more rules and laws to ensure that even when circumstances present a choice of doing the right thing or the wrong thing, all the people born as good, always choose the right thing. Indicates that, all people born 'as good' need to be coerced to continue to be 'good'.

The question then is about, can people born 'as good' punish the one who under the pressure of circumstances chose to do 'the wrong thing'? Let's say a person born 'as good' under the pressure of circumstances commits an act of murder, now other people also born 'as good' decide to punish this choice made by the person. Let's assume he is awarded the capital punishment. Won't this mean that collectively a group of people who are born 'as good' under the pressure of circumstances decided to do the 'wrong thing' namely, killing the person who chose to do 'the wrong thing'. Can we call that just, acceptable or civilized? Can two wrongs make a right? ***Interestingly, 18th Century French philosopher Jean Jacques Rousseau, said 'we are born with a conscience and a sense of fairness. Human nature is good until corrupted by society.***

**So how much responsibility is the society willing to take collectively? Can there be true Justice?**

# Just is Still Complicated

Justice and Punishment are they one and the same. In order for Justice to be done has punishment got to be given? There are three objectives that the current system of justice tries to achieve:

- Retribution
- Deterrence
- Reformation

As was discussed in the past two blogs [Just is Complicated | Just is as Complicated], with much arbitration and debate a punishment is given to a person indicted in an undesirable act or crime. In the process of awarding such punishment, the objective of retribution is to some extent met however; it is the objective of deterrence and reformation that this process fails in.

In the previous two blogs I tried to explore the question of Justice with the assumption of either we are born evil or we are born 'as good'. They both led to interesting outcomes. I now think, after further contemplation that, we are born neither good nor bad. The whole matter is about conflict of interest and intent.

- Interest of an individual vs. Interest of another individual
- Interest of a State vs. Interest of an individual

- Interest of a State vs. Interest of another State
- Interest of a corporate vs. interest of an individual
- Interest of a corporate vs. Interest of another corporate

So on and so forth. It is during this conflict of interest that we seek arbitration of a third party hoping through their unbiased and neutral stand point they might be able to decide whose Interest/Intent appears as most noble and justified. There are some widely accepted moral mores and ethics of human behavior which are to some extent influenced by religion and something that is not easy to be defined in exact terms. These, somewhat tacit, morals and ethics form the base of many law formulations and attempt to resolve conflict of interest or intent.

This could lead to quite a confusing notion of Justice. Taking an extreme example, wars are not illegal. In an armed conflict, killing of opposition's army personnel is not illegal. However any attempts of killing civilians or torturing captured soldiers is considered a crime. If the moral and ethics drive our idea of justice then, any form of killing should have been illegal, hence war should have been illegal and hence Armed forces should have been illegal and hence the Government that maintains them should have been illegal!

I think what emerges is that in an ***institutionalized justice system***. It comes in only when a conflict of interest is reported, till it is reported and not legislated against, all acts are legal and absolutely moral and ethical. Hence I think retribution is relatively easy (note the word relatively) compared to deterrence or reformation.

# To Do or Not to Do

"*To be, or not to be*" is the opening phrase of a soliloquy in William Shakespeare's play Hamlet, I would say often the dilemma is not as much to BE but of DO. So my opening phrase would have been '*To Do or not To Do*'. The dilemma of 'to do or not to do' could pretty strongly influence 'to be or not to be'. My observation indicates 'To be or not to Be' is often a matter of chance but 'To do or not to do' is always a matter of choice. Sometimes it is similar to that of throwing a dice, the choice is only of throwing or not throwing, once thrown one is at the mercy of the outcome and has to bear it's consequences.

I guess it is the ***fear of the consequences*** that puts one in a dilemma of 'To do or not to do', one is sometimes lost in the 'what ifs' and shies away from 'To Do'. Some instances one throws the dice but refuse to own the outcome. Apart from outcome of the 'Do', even the dilemma itself could be overwhelming and people could become depressed, hysterical or disillusioned as sometimes 'Not to Do' could also be the right thing to do! Nonetheless, nobody is ever completely free from the dilemma. Infact I would say that 'To Be' would often and invariably lead to occasions in life where the 'To Do or not To Do' is unavoidable. I guess there are only two ways to deal with it, think through the situation like a chess player before you move/do or instinctively throw the dice like a gambler, but in either situations be ready to get surprised.

Recently I saw two movies that beautifully highlighted both the dilemma. It manages to bring out the dilemma and how the decision in either direction has strong consequences.

The first one called '12 Angry Men'. depicts how a small doubt in the mind of one of a 12 man jury converts a 11:1 in favor of Guilty is converted to 12:0 in favor of not-guilty. Yes the movie itself is very beautifully shot with characters that we could relate to, however importantly it holds up some interesting questions of

> *How our personal belief and bias influences decision making.*
> *How we often pay less attention to the consequence of our decision even if it was costing somebody their life.*
> *How a simple dispassionate and logical probe could lay open our vulnerability.*

The second one called 'The Ox Bow Incident'. is completely in contrast to the one I described above. The movie depicts how inspite of there being sufficient doubts and no eye witness an angry mob themselves believe three people to be guilty and decide to take the law in their hand and kill them, without a fair trial, only to discover that they were wrong! There were voices of dissent in the mob but they were stifled to submission by the majority. Again a very beautifully made movie with characters that we could recognise and also possibly identify with. the question of

> '*To do or not to do*' and also

if 'to do' then '*what to do*' and how do we decide what to do.

***When we decide is that purely logical thinking based on facts or does it have our accumulated, emotions, view points and bias that influence what we decide***, also when we decide do we really think about the ***repercussion*** of that on people around us

These may appear to be rather isolated incidents, from the point of view of the circumstances under which these movies are set. However there is a larger question. the question of '***To do or not to do***' and also if 'to do' then '***what to do***' and how do we decide what to do. ***When we decide is that purely logical thinking based on facts or does it have our accumulated, emotions, view points and bias that influence what we decide***, also when we decide do we really think about the ***repercussion*** of that on people around us? I invite you to view these movies at leisure and enjoy the contrasting viewpoints they depict.

# Curious case of a Rapist

## 22 *Saturday* Sep 2012

Rape is undoubtedly one of the most heinous crimes against woman in any country. Strict laws exist in all countries to act as a deterrent for any perpetrator, though there are incidents of rape that keep getting reported quite regularly. I would like to argue that the convicted rapist is only a scapegoat in such incidents, the real culprit is the society. The society in order to prove itself innocent ensures that either the charges are convicted or are proved baseless. All this is done with due diligence to prove how just and prompt the society is, yet it can't get rid itself of the guilt each time such an act happens.

The male of any species is entrusted with a basic instinct to mate and pro-create, the female of any species possess methods of attracting the right male for the purpose of mating so that the species could survive and sustain. In animals the act is rather mechanical and also indiscrete and promiscuous, some of the tribals around the world are also known for that. The so called civilised society, in a way, has been about, effort to curb and rein in the promiscuity involved in the act of pro-creation and give it a more decent form. While one must say that the promiscuity has been curbed or camouflaged to a large extent, however not much has been done to modify the basic instincts. What also doesn't help is the civilised society's obsession with the female form.

It is rather surprising element of a civilised society, while acts of sexual crime are condemned yet the obsession with the female form goes on unabated. One look at our literature, print media, audio-visual media, entertainment industry will show how strongly are we obsessed with it. Both classical and contemporary literature have played a strong role in fueling and sustaining this obsession, interesting description and newer ways of describing the female form has been appreciated. While the artistic expression, undoubtedly, has to be appreciated yet their indirect contribution to sustaining the obsession with female form of the society as a whole cannot be ignored. Same could be said about the other forms of media who have constantly fueled it and do so even to the current day.

The obsession of the male towards the subject could be said to be conscious lecherousness and unconscious attempt to find appropriate partner, the female obsession towards the matter is out of insecurity, inadequacy or opportunity. The extent to which the female form is used repeatedly and with uncurbed exaggeration that it has a constant presence in the unconscious of everyone of the members of the civilised society. So, on one hand the male basic instinct has not changed and on the other hand the obsession with the female form continues unabated, both of this put together form a potent combination and a festering ground for heinous crime and oppression. No wonder from time to time we see the unwanted "Dress Codes" being specified for female students, professionals or citizens and that is considered as one of the reasons for the crime.

I feel instigated to say that civilised society in the attempt to curb promiscuity has let loose a demon that it didn't know existed. So much so that I would not hesitate to state that all of the males of a civilised society is a potential rapist, though the one that actually trips the rope is the convict and if the charges are proved the whole society doesn't spare in making the person feel unwanted and a bane to the human life. Yet the trap was already set and the act played out intelligently to hide the real motive.

Unless society collectively learns to get rid of this obsession of the female form and the male basic instinct to pro-create could be transformed, I would say that we haven't yet seen the end of the heinous crimes against woman no matter how much modern and technologically advanced world we might consider ourselves to be. I understand that Individuals make the society but after the society is formed the society now starts defining the individual. So change has to come from individuals and slowly propagate to cover the whole society.

# GoWhereMeant

Who or What is the Government? Is it the bureaucracy? Is it the cabinet? Is it the Prime Minister? Is the President? Is it the Constitution?

We would all agree, I suppose, that the Bureaucracy and cabinet are nothing but a set of musical chairs with the occupants changing, moving and shifting. They are entrusted to execute duties of a Government but are not Government unto themselves. Then what is the Government? The Prime Minister or the President are not The Government either, they are at best leaders, protectors or saviors of one. Then, is the constitution the Government? Certainly the Constitution of any country lays the foundation of how the Government should function but again is not the Government per se. Even if it was, the Constitution, at the very core, is nothing more than a Concept, a concept proposed by the founding fathers of any state and ratified by consensus. *So, I conclude that, Government is nothing more than just a concept!* The rest of the paraphernalia we call, the ministry or bureaucracy or armed forces are only to protect and give continuity to this concept.

Undoubtedly, this is a very powerful concept that we all believe in and willingly submit to. Our link to this concept is similar to the thin rope that prevents an adult elephant from escaping. Because the Government is just a concept, it is open to many interpretations. Some form of interpretation has led to violence and atrocities which are, in a way, acts of terror. Instances of people being accused for sedition or getting arrested for FB posts, or for more benign acts are victims of this act of terror. Why do we surrender our authority to Governments when we don't know what or who the Government is? Why do we, so called common man, surrender our empowerment so willingly to the safeguards of a Concept?

A concept, can't give legitimacy to people. It is people who give legitimacy to a concept. Like all of us have given to Government and entrusted it with enormous power my surrendering our individual powers. Without the legitimacy, the taxes that we pay are in no way different than rents paid to mafia. Here, I think, there is merit in the idea of <u>Voluntary Taxation</u> regime where, I should have the ***right to protest by refusing to pay tax*** or have the ***option to pay taxes only for a particular cause***. If I am being forced to pay taxes, I fail to see the difference between Government and a Mafia. Anyway no matter what Mafia still exists due to flaws in the existing Concept.

The moot point is that, it is 'WE' who matter; it is 'WE' who give power to Governments and it can never be the other way round. Government is just a concept, morality and ethics don't apply to a concept, it only applies to people who form that concept like us. We have the power to make changes. Unless we standup and make those changes ourselves nothing concrete will happen. ***I am sure we don't believe ourselves to be criminals waiting to commit crimes if not supervised, and can decide and act as per what is the right thing to do.***

# Double Jeopardy

## <u>12 *Wednesday* Jun 2013</u>

A modern society has been constructed. It is promoted as a panacea for all the major problems that plague mankind. Also, right from abolition of slavery to invention of cutting edge technology, has all been attributed to be fruits of modern society; the obvious question that arises is that, how does a modern society differ from a traditional society? While this might not find a very convincing answer, however, for ease of differentiation and ease of explanation it is largely accepted that a society constructed on the tenets of industrialization is a modern society and a society that is still based on agrarian economy is a traditional or orthodox society. The sole aim of a modern society is poverty alleviation.

Poverty is considered as the biggest curse to mankind and also the root of most evil. Alleviating poverty has been identified as one of the key markers of a modern society. Industrialization, due to its capacity to employ people in large numbers and due to high productivity, is suggested as the most effective method to fight poverty. European countries (read Great Britain) were the pioneers of industrialization and contributed vastly in the construction of a modern society. Anti-thesis to this is an agrarian society or a society based on agriculture. As agriculture is a low productive activity, it is considered incapable of addressing poverty. Hence, the west has developed a modern society on the basis of rapid and large scale industrialization. Such is the belief of West on this form of society that, it is portrayed and promoted as a 'model' for all other non-industrialized countries to follow.

An Industrialized society is highly dependent on availability of natural resources. Natural resources include – oil, gas, coal, water and man power. Also the economy of an industrialized modern society is very complicated in nature. With the discontinuation of the Gold Standard post WW II the modern society largely relies on complicated calculations by central banks in deciding how much money should be in circulation. Circulation just sufficient enough to

Keep the economy growing but keep cost of goods within acceptable limits. It is absolutely essential for the economy of a modern society to keep growing; this ensures a constant increase in jobs and more opportunities for people earn their way out of poverty and at the same time they could help in sustaining growth.

Interestingly, the observation across the world has been that, the massive industrialization undertaken by a modern society has led to an unsustainable growth pattern. The growth has put stress on natural resources. The excessive use of natural resources is causing irreversible impact on the atmosphere and supposedly contributing to climate change. Another observation about industrialized economies is that it is not only money in circulation that decides growth or robustness of an economy, but also who is spending. Excessive government spending leads to imbalances that often reflect as fiscal deficit and excessive spending by private sector leads to increase in prices; finding a balance has proven to be tough and stressful. To strike a balance many governments go on an austerity drive, many private organization go on the course of retrenchment. Both of these efforts have adverse effect on jobs and leads to massive unemployment. Unemployment fosters poverty. In some instances extreme poverty also becomes root cause for crimes.

Thus the vicious cycle continues. A quest of modern society to be able to fuel growth without jeopardizing natural resources or the environment and yet cater to the needs of the growing human population. Inspite of millions of years of existence and couple of centuries of industrialization mankind has not managed to wipe out poverty. In some instances it almost feels that poverty is an essential aspect of human existence just to prove that human spirit can triumph over any adversity. Also with the new levels of requirements (greed) getting added to Human needs, poverty itself is becoming a moving concept. So the well-off of yesterday could be the new pauper of tomorrow! Without even analyzing the merits of a traditional society, I just wonder how sustainable is this modern society and by rapid multiplication of human population and following industrialization as an essential method of poverty alleviation, whether mankind has failed itself.

# Modern Orthodoxy

## <u>19</u> *Friday* **Apr 2013**

We say we live in modern times and we call ourselves modern. I keep wondering what we do that is radically different from our previous generation or the one before that which gives us a reason to call ourselves modern. **Oxford dictionary gives the definition of the word Modern** *as a person who advocates or practises a departure from traditional styles or values*. I am speaking in a contemporary context. Have we really departed from traditional styles and values of the past two generations to call ourselves modern? If yes then, what styles and values have we moved away from?

When we look at our lives there is a cyclical nature to it and also presence of a strong pattern:

- • - Everybody earns for living
- • - Everybody has relationships
- • - Everybody has kids
- • - Everybody has ups and downs in life
- • - Everybody worry for their kids
- • - Everybody looks towards their kids marriage
- • - Everybody has sensual pleasures
- • - Everybody has fears

When we face a particular situation it appears as if we are the only one caught in such a situation and struggle through it cursing this world to have put us through such an ordeal. However when we open up to people about our problems, not only do we realize that others have faced similar situations we also realize how trivial our situation appears in comparison to that of somebody else. This either makes us realize our folly in feeling we have a huge problem on hand or gives us the courage to face our problems on our own. However there is nothing new in this, both the situation and problems appear repetitive and cyclical in nature when, we take the entire mankind into account. Fundamental problems of human life and living remain unresolved as we get to embroiled and held up with seemingly insurmountable problems of our lives.

With a strong prevalence of institutionalization, we have entrusted various institutions with the responsibility of solving fundamental problems of human living. Spiritual is left to the religious institutions, gathering skills to earn a living to Education institutions, law and order to judicial institutions, politics to the institution of government and so on and so forth. Once such entrusting has been completed what is left of our lives? We are ready to be totally embroiled in the day to day trivial problems of our lives and unconsciously allow the institutions to dictate terms to us.

So the question arises – how are we modern? Does use of technology makes us modern? Does the entrusting of responsibilities to various institutions make us modern? Does our dressing sense makes us modern? What traditional styles and values have we really departed from to call ourselves modern?

**George Orewell** says

*"Orthodoxy means not thinking–not needing to think. Orthodoxy is unconsciousness."*

*"To exchange one orthodoxy for another is not necessarily an advance. The enemy is the gramophone mind, whether or not one agrees with the record that is being played at the moment."*

# It's Not Word It

*The word is not the thing* – said **Alfred Korzybski.**

Homo sapiens learnt and unlearnt many skills as they evolved into civilized social animals. Language is one such learnt skill that has evolved over a period of time from its humble beginning of incoherent grunts. As the experience of homo-sapiens became richer the need for an evolved linguistic tool must have become that much more evident. In order to communicate coherently more structured and logical linguistic tools evolved and took the shape of full-fledged languages with well defined syntax and semantics. For every experience there seemed to be a linguistic representation in the form of a matching word. Consistent usage of words gave it continuity and a permanent place in our memory.

Today language is an essential aspect of everybody's growing-up process. Today, it won't be wrong to say that, as a grown up, we see our experiences and situations through a mesh of words and linguistic tools. We recognize a situation only through words and our strength of vocabulary. However, every word suffers from a shortcoming. *The shortcoming is of, its usage being subject to an individual's interpretation. There are plenty of assumptions as well. I'd like to argue that, today we humans are so adept with words that we never come directly in touch with our experience or situations. Most of the times we only come in touch with the word that we decide to call that experience by.*

For example in a relationship – what we like and whatever makes us feel good, feel beautiful and feel ecstatic– we call it LOVE. So we are not directly experiencing the feeling but are experiencing it through the word LOVE. The moment something unfavorable happens, when we recognize it is not what we used to call LOVE, and react differently. Thus the word and its limitation dictates what we eventually experience and hence how we react. We are stuck in dealing with the word and try to bucket similar experiences under the word.

One might counter argue saying that, our learning is through these words, it is these words that give us the clarity in understanding and hence our knowledge. While I understand the basis of such an argument, however I also think that it raises a serious epistemological question. As I see it, we experience and learn about the world in two ways – i] sensual (through our senses) and ii] through language. The latter is supposed to be a secondary method through which we make it easier to comprehend what we learn through the former. However, *I feel, in due course we experience everything sensual through a mesh of words and thus making our sensual experience a secondary method. Here-in our learning and our reaction to situations become erratic and incoherent.*

# Einstein's Dice

*"God doesn't play dice with the universe"* Is a popular quote by the great scientist of 20th Century **Albert Einstein**. Einstein was among select few of popular personalities, whose fame transcended the boundaries of the field that they worked in. He is still quoted widely by people in fields other than physics, and in certain occasions misquoted as well.

Einstein's belief in God was a point of discussion throughout his life and he had to give statements to clarify what his beliefs really were about the matter. I found it quite interesting to know that Einstein's famous quote 'God doesn't play dice with the universe' is often used to highlight his belief in God and belief in a pre-determined destiny. It is often used to support arguments in favor of presence of God and of human destiny. Contrary to popular belief though, the statement was made neither out of faith in God nor out of belief in pre-determined destiny. In fact it was made out of desperation.

In early 20th century when scientific activity was at its peak, the likes of Max Planck, Albert Einstein, Niels Bohr, Erwin Schrodinger, Werner Heisenberg and many more, were slowly but surely moving away from the concept of a deterministic Newtonian world. What an amazing era it must have been -to witness great brains fighting it out to make sense of the baffling world of sub-atomic particles and Quantum

Physics. At this time, Einstein was at logger heads with Niels Bohr. Experiments by physicists related to sub-atomic particles and their quantum states had not only raised many questions but also left many unanswered. Attempt to answer some of them was made in 1927 at Copenhagen, by all the great physicists of the time; *Copenhagen Interpretation*. This discussion was inconclusive and it divided the physicists' world over; on one side was *Einstein who was unable to accept the subjective nature of matter (wave – particle duality) and the other side was Neils Bohr who was able to accept the uncertain and subjective nature of matter.*

Einstein would spend the rest of his life to try and prove his point and attempt to come up with a unified theory. A theory that could combine his theory of Relativity (about to large Celestial bodies) with Quantum Theory (about tiny sub-atomic particles) and resolve unanswered questions. It was out of this desperation of being unable to comprehend the indeterministic nature of matter that, Einstein cried out – 'God doesn't play dice with the universe'. This, inspite of the fact that, he didn't believe in the concept of a personal God who watches over the world and works on a principle of reward or punishment. He believed in the monist philosophy popularized by Spinoza and a mystical connection of matter and thought and oneness of soul and body. *Contrastingly however, the quote has often been misquoted to indicate that even a great mind like Einstein did believe in the existence of God!* Infact on various occasions Einstein has described himself as agnostic bordering on athiesm: *Einstein stated: "I have repeatedly said that in my opinion the idea of a personal God is a childlike one. You may call me an agnostic, but I do not share the crusading spirit of the professional atheist whose fervor is mostly due to a painful act of liberation from the fetters of religious indoctrination received in youth. I prefer an attitude of humility corresponding to the weakness of our intellectual understanding of nature and of our own being."*

# Plateau and Beyond

## <u>10 *Saturday* **Aug 2013**</u>

When Lance Armstrong after years of speculation came out and confessed about doping the whole world reacted with shock and disappointment. The downfall of an inspirational figure in world sport was both disheartening and disappointing. He was severely criticized and stripped of all his tour de France victories. In lieu of the recent spate of doping scandals arising across the world, however, raises a question of whether we reacted unfairly towards Lance Armstrong?

Look at the recent cases of doping issue:

- French Hurdler Decaux banned for doping Aug 2013
- Belarus Shot putter Andrei Mikhnevich fails dope test Aug 2013
- American Major league Baseball star Alex Rodriguez was banned for 211 games for doping Aug 2013
- American athlete Tyson Gay and Jamaican athlete Asafa Powell fail dope test July 2013
- Indian shot putter P Udai Laxmi fails dope test – withdrawn from Asian Championship July 2013
- Australian Cricket Board accepts to systemic problem of Doping Jun 2013

While the respective governing bodies have taken appropriate action against the faltering individuals – but I think it raises deep questions that probably are disheartening to find answers for.

## Have we as humans hit a plateau with respect to our athletic ability?

On 6th May 1954 Roger Banister for the first time ran a mile under 4 minutes. In many ways he liberated our minds in what was possible and set the tone for some awe inspiring performances. We have seen plenty of world records being bettered over the years. It made us believe it is ***mind over matter*** and whatever the mind can conceive the body can achieve. Thus far it has proven to be true and many athletes stand testimony to it. Logically thinking though – there has to be a limit to how far we could push our body. At one point we probably would reach the top of the plateau despite all the power of our innovative imagination. Have we reached that point? Have we hit that plateau? Has our physiology finally known its limit?

As far as track and field events are concerned will the World Records that stand as of today ever be bettered again? Bettered to what extent? What's the price of such an endeavor and can it be done with natural athletic ability? Or can our psychology continue to influence physiology and push the boundary further away? The recent doping incidents do indicate in a sense that what the mind is conceiving the body is desperately trying to achieve but failing without the banned supplements to reach there.

## If we have hit a plateau – when did we hit it?

If we have really hit the plateau – when did we hit it? Ben Johnson in 1988 was stripped of his Olympic Gold when he was found guilty of doping. Lance Armstrong confessed of doping as early as 1992-93. Are all these indications that the level of performances we desire to see are possible only if one doped? Did we hit the plateau long ago and some unlucky people got caught of using performance enhancing drugs while others who were not enjoyed public adulation?

In 2002 Jeffrey Archer published series of books based on a diary that he wrote while serving his prison sentence. In one of these books he talks about how prisoners used to get high on various drugs but also knew how to flush it out of the system before the prison Dr examined them. When prisoners could figure this out how difficult would it be for athletes, who have access to world class medical facility and consultation, to figure out? It's scary to think on these lines and demoralizing as well, however it stares at our face waiting to gain our attention.

## Are we pushing our athletes to inhuman levels?

The other point also is that sports from being past time activities and modes of keeping the human body tuned have become a profession by themselves. Sports are now the exclusive domain of professional athletes and some are handsomely paid for it as well. *It is as if, many of us have outsourced our share of athletic performance and burdened the shoulders of the professional athletes*. It is a vicarious experience of whatever natural athletic ability all of us possess and also provides us with entertainment. In this process have we overburdened the professional athletes?

Any professional athlete, apart from his, also shoulders the expectation and aspiration of others. The expectation is of peak performance and at a very rapid interval for an athlete to linger in people's mind and earn a living. In this process have we pushed them so far that they have no option but to do whatever is required to stay away from injuries and perform at extreme pressure situation? Some who do resort to doping are more of a victim while they might appear to be benefiting from it.

## What is Natural Ability in sport?

On the other hand one might also question whether sport has ever been a level playing field that it claims to be. There are sportsmen with a specific genetic disposition for a particular game; developed countries with better sports infrastructure also manage to provide their athletes with better dietary supplements. Ofcourse there is always an anti-thesis to this and Jesse Owens in 1932 Berlin Olympics not only proved Hitler wrong but was the most successful athlete of the games! One might argue that the level to which professional sports have risen, it is absolutely mandatory to have essential and acceptable dietary supplements apart from having a flair for the sport. The players who can't afford them are at an obvious disadvantage; however this is not treated as an unfair competitive advantage as doping is. Also people have argued that people who think that certain drugs that act as performance enhancers don't in anyway enhance the players skills – so whether we should make doping legal?

Many questions but no answers in sight, there are points and counter-points but no consensus. Till we re-think how we view professional sports players resorting to doping would continue to be castigated. ***Will psychology continue to triumph over any obvious physiological limits as it has done so far?***

# I am Poor

## 24 *Saturday* Aug 2013

India is recognized worldwide as to be the home of some the world's poorest of people. Reduction of poverty levels has been treated as the primary goal for all the activities undertaken by the Government. In this regards, there has been a raging debate on the claim of the current government about drastic reduction in poverty levels. This tricky and controversial topic attracted my attention and I found myself at loss about whether or not to believe the Government on this. As with most issues the Government and Opposition get busy throwing brickbats at each other without bothering to explain the problem at hand to the citizens a. I decide to explore this independently.

Key to any exploration or learning is to ask the right questions. Starting at that –

What is Poverty?
How do we define Poverty?
Who is responsible for Poverty?
Who should act to reduce Poverty?
Why should we measure Poverty?
How can we measure poverty?
What steps could be taken to reduce Poverty?
**What is Poverty? How to Define Poverty?**

"**I am poor**" does this statement make any sense? In our day to day conversation most of us have used this phrase in various situations. What did it mean? Did it mean we don't earn enough to afford what we want to have? Or did it mean what we earn was not sufficient to buy what we think we ought to have for a dignified living? Is poverty a result of what we earn or is it a result of what we can't afford? Or is it a result of not having access to certain essential resources that assist one in earning an income that in turn allows them to afford the amenities required for a dignified living? How do we decide what we "ought to have" and what "dignified living is"? Both of these concepts being very subjective means that no two people would agree on their respective definition of "**being poor**".

Some factors emerge from the above short inquiry. First that Poverty seems to have three components and one characteristic

- • - Income
- • - Deprivation of resources
- • - Lack of dignity
- • - Relativeness

It appears to be an uphill task to come to a common ground on defining

- Below what income would one be qualified as poor
- Deprivation of what resources leads to poverty
- What is dignified living
- An agreeable definition that is consistent across societies/countries

Economists and Sociologists around the world have spent many hours in taking one or two of the above points and drawing up a definition of poverty. Needless to say that each is as controversial as the other and can be proved wrong on many counts.

## Who or What is Responsible for Poverty?

It is tough to understand why there is poverty. We know that resources are always limited and the fight is to find out an appropriate method of distribution of resources among all the people. There seems to be an inherent characteristic in all our social systems since time immemorial that, it always has certain segment of people relatively deprived than the others. I don't know what to attribute this characteristic to, however it is always there. One might argue that when it is a natural outcome of every social system then why bother about it? While a convincing logical answer might be tough to find, I think that human existence and superiority of human race over other animals would be questioned if obvious disparities are not eradicated. It is a collective responsibility of all the people to fight and work towards systems that assist people to live the way one would want to.

## Why should we measure Poverty?

In this regards one might ask what should one do to alleviate the situation. I think there are three important aspects. One – to find what are the absolute necessities to live a dignified life; Second – through consensus, find what percentage of people are deprived of these absolute necessities; Third – is to give the people that fall under this targeted category, a chance to decide if they indeed want to be called poor. Forcibly including people contented with their living and exposing them to unknown levels of living is, I think, a way to induce poverty where none existed. It is to deal with arguments like these that the need to measure poverty arose. Also countries those are serious about alleviating poverty and providing access to resources for the majority of their population, would like to know how many people are deprived so policies could be devised accordingly.

**How can we measure Poverty?**

There are many measurement methods proposed, used, reworked, discarded and continuously debated to understand what is poverty and how many people could be called poor. People have used the following parameters:

- - Income
- - Calorie Intake
- - Income and a feel if this income allows people to live the life they want to
- - Access to basic amenities

Due to subjectivity of the matter it is very tough to define in absolute terms who are and who are not poor. People might also feel insulted if one is called poor by someone. Yet to devise policies that would positively impact people suffering from adverse living conditions, there is a need to identify how many fall in this deprived category. Also there is a need to measure poverty in absolute terms. There are many global bodies such as World Bank and International Monetary Fund who have taken responsibility, for reasons best known to them, to alleviate poverty at international level. In order to allocate funds or grants or loans to countries to assist them in their respective fight against poverty, they need to know in relative terms which country is worse off than the other. Here United Nation Development Program through various research methodologies arrived at the $1.25 as the bare minimum income that is essential for a decent survival. Anyone earning below this income is considered to be living in absolute poverty. Needless to say that any poverty line is sensitive to inflation levels existing in each country.

## Steps to Reduce Poverty?

Alleviating poverty is a tricky business. Firstly one must understand that alleviating poverty is not in any form similar to giving alms to beggars. Infact giving money to the poor with the view of alleviating poverty snatches away the right to dignified living. Any policy of this nature would prove to be counterproductive and detrimental in the process of poverty alleviation. Being poor is subjective and not only depends on how much one earns but also on what one aspires to have. Governments have to play a role in ensuring stable prices of essential food items and also ensure accessibility to resources (ex. Finance) that could assist people to find ways to earn more. Also in countries where there is stigma attached to people born in certain communities, access to sources of income or resources is itself very difficult task, in such cases ghetto mentality keeps one deeply rooted in the state of poverty one might want to desperately escape from. Rapid economic growth has been championed as the best way to alleviate poverty, undoubtedly it has played a positive role, however where the stigma is attached with where one is born it becomes more complicated to address the problem of poverty.

# Progressive Dilemma

## 13 *Friday* Sep 2013

If we accept Darwin's theory of evolution we would have to agree that human life has been a constant endeavor to evolve and be civilized. While physical evolution has been incidental, it is the psychological evolvement that we consciously endeavor for in all aspects of life. Psychological evolution presents many epistemological and methodological challenges. For example the idea of justice and equality, I think, has been the toughest idea to comprehend and bring consensus on.

The gruesome crime committed on 16th of December 2012 in Delhi has brought many such fundamental questions back on the discussion table. The spontaneous eruption of countrywide protests in the aftermath of the incident and continuous ongoing reports of heinous crimes against women has shaken everybody's conscience and also questioned the very essence of humanity in many ways. Once such a crime as rape is committed what could possibly be the appropriate punishment for the convicts of the crime? What if the convict is a juvenile? If the rape victim survives what is the appropriate method of rehabilitating and restoring her dignity and honor?

Apart from these, I think, the issue also raises questions about how much of importance our society gives to forgiveness, reformation, genuine repentance and reintegration of a convicted criminal back into society. Every religion has given prime importance to the concept of forgiveness and repentance however as a society we humans appear to be quite intolerant towards both these factors. Infact no forgiveness or repentance ever appear to be complete, genuine or unconditional, nor is there a way to measure if we have reached the desired level with respect to either of these qualities. Also criminals present a very unique dilemma – they are a burden on the society no matter where they are, whether as part of regular society, as they could cause irreparable damage, or as prisoners locked up in a prison, as they then become beneficiary of a system that is created out of our pockets. At the same time psychologically death penalty or capital punishment has been something that many want to do away with and awarding of such a punishment has been viewed as a mark of backwardness.

The more I think of it the more complicated the matter gets and all solution seem wrong and right at the same time! I guess this is what will keep us humans in the 'Work in Progress' bracket and hope that with psychological evolution we make better choices among the contradictory tradeoffs.

# Intuition or Coercion

## 15 *Tuesday* Oct 2013

Is it Intuition or Coercion? We often talk about certain insight we get about possible unfavorable or favorable future occurrences which tend to mould our present actions. We tend to call such foresight as Intuition. Are these intuitions entirely independent and uninfluenced by our thought process? I attempted a short exercise to see if this could be understood.

| Me | Event | Foresight | Outcome | Conclusion |
|----|-------|-----------|---------|------------|
| 0 | 0 | 0 | Pure Observer, non predictable future event, no foresight | |
| 0 | 0 | 1 | Pure Observer, Non predictable future event, pure foresight | Pure Intuition |
| 0 | 1 | 0 | Pure Observer. Desired future event, no foresight | |
| 0 | 1 | 1 | Pure Observer, Desired future event, foresight | Partially induced Intuition |
| 1 | 0 | 0 | Creator, Non predictable future event, no foresight | |
| 1 | 0 | 1 | Creator, Non predictable future event, foresight | Partially induced Intuition |
| 1 | 1 | 0 | Creator, Desired future event, no foresight | |
| 1 | 1 | 1 | Creator, Desired future event, foresight | Pure Coercion |

| Legend | |
|--------|--------------------------|
| 0 | pure observer |
| 1 | Creator |
| 0 | Non predictable future event |
| 1 | desired future event |
| 0 | No foresight |
| 1 | Foresight |

There are three factors as I see.
- Me who could either be a Pure Observer or a Creator
- Event The event about which I could have a foresight
  - o Event could be a desired event or completely unpredictable event
- Foresight -the foresight itself

Only one of the many possible outcomes appears to be what could really be called intuition. Rest all leave sufficient space for doubt whether our thought process was involved in anyway and the foresight was a continuation of the long desired goal/target. Should we take more responsibility of what happens to us rather than act victim?

# PnP Legacy

**Psychology over Physiology or Physiology over Psychology**. This question has always intrigued me. Man is a sum of his Physiology and Psychology, however the question is whether both are important in equal proportion or does one dominate over the other.

Modern history of mankind is full of instances where some obvious physical shortcomings were overcome by strong psychological resolve. Yet during moments of physical illness we must have observed its impact on our mental health. Again, many doctors indicate that recovery from illness varies from person to person due to difference in respective psychological make-up. The one with strongest psychological resolve demonstrates capability of not only recovering fast but sometimes even recovering from a hopeless terminal illness. **Louise Hayhouse** is one such example. This sort of tilts the balance in favor of Psychology.

**Hellen Keller** was born with some very severe physical disabilities because of which she suffered from severe psychological issues. Yet it was her psychological resolve that helped her overcome her disabilities and become an icon that she eventually became. There was also the case of **Dr Roger Bannister** who for the first time in the history of mankind ran a mile under 4 mins. One could possibly argue that his particular physical disposition made it possible to do so;

237

however the fact that after him people have continued to break that barrier till it stopped being a barrier anymore indicates something that happened beyond the physical realm.

At this stage Psychology seems to be asserting its dominance over physiology. Let me see if we could even things out. Physical damage to brain has been known to have severe impact on a person's psychology. Genetics also has been found to have its say and no amount of psychological resolve has been effectively proven to have any impact on it. As the physical health fails through life the psychological resolve also demonstrates a similar decline. Yet there have been many instances where perfectly healthy and physically fit individual go through phases of deep depression and psychological disorder. One could argue that a person who does rigorous physical activity or exercise aids release of a certain hormone that helps in keeping depression or stress at bay. Yet suicide among Indian farmers is so common. Nobody could possibly be working physically as harder as a farmer yet some seemingly insurmountable barrier pushes him to suicide. Also the moment a physical exercise or activity to improve psychological well-being is proposed it sort of points out which is the means and which is the ends. Then again physical exercise is prescribed just for physical well-being as well.

Roman poet **Juvenal** wrote the famous words *mens sana in corpore sano* which translated to English means **Healthy Mind in a Healthy Body**. However he didn't indicate which the pre-condition is. Even **Vivekananda**, a person known to have delved the depths of psychological world advised people to maintain a healthy body as 'that' he says 'is the essential instrument provided to man through which one could exert control over mental faculties'. Much like the chicken and egg question this debate about dominance of psychology or physiology suffers from a circular argument.

The only conclusion that I am able to draw is that Psychology is dominant and has the power to overcome obvious Physiological shortcomings only if the physiology is at a certain optimal level. Best of physical conditioning fails to prevent psychological imbalances or disorder. The balance seems to be firmly shifting in favor of Psychology.

# Walk of Life

When we talk about Hinduism there are many images that come flooding in our mind, millions of Gods, rites, rituals, sages and many more. Yet there are many people who would say it is not a religion, it's a way of life that it doesn't even have a name and the name that everything within the religion is symbolic. I wonder if there is any truth in these popular notions when like any other religion it is now institutionalized and riddled with malpractices, superstitions and shortcomings.

I present a short sequence of thoughts and findings to see what it could possibly be.

**Universality of Caste System:**

The moment discussion on Hinduism starts there are immediate questions raised about caste, caste system and the related oppression of certain class of people. I think these are misinterpretations that creep into popular practice and public psyche and develop strong inertia towards change. I quote two slokas or verses from the Bhagwad Gita and the Rig Veda, two books that are sacred to the followers of this religion.

*In Bhagwad Gita Chapter 4 verse 13 Krishna says:*

*Catur-varnyam maya sristam guna-karma-vibhagasah,*

Which means, '**the four varnas were created by me and they are divisions based on qualities (Guna) and actions (Karma) of a person**' the caste of a person will be decided on the basis of his character and action and not by birth!

*Athreya Smrithi Book 5 of Rig Veda says:*
*janmana jayate sudrah*
*samskarad bhaved dvijah*
*veda-pathad bhaved vipro*
*brahma janatiti brahmanah*

*Which means 'everybody is born a Sudra (lowest caste), one who follows the samskaras or right action and thoughts one becomes re-born (dvijah), the one who reads the vedas becomes a learned person (vipra/vipro) and only the one who gains knowledge of the ultimate truth (Brahma or Brahman) becomes a Brahmin (brahmanah).*

*These two interesting verses from the two of the most sacred books indeed bring out a universality of the philosophical thoughts embedded in them*

### *The Trigunas*

*Exploring further, there are three primary gunas or qualities identified –*

**Rajas** *– characterized by high energy levels, desires, passion, action, result oriented, industriousness*

**Tamas** – *characterized by indolence, laziness, lack of motivation, lack of desire*

**Sattva** – *Characterized by spiritual bent of mind, impassioned work, higher energy level, calmness, quiet confidence*

*I guess it isn't difficult to see that men and women that demonstrate one or two or all three of such gunas, spans over all religious, geographical or political boundaries.*

### Universality in the stages of human life:

*Furthering the understanding of the human behavior and the needs scriptures identify the need for a balanced life. Both material well-being and spiritual well-being are given equal importance. Thus the life span of a human is divided into stages.*

**Brahmacharya** – *the age of learning, accumulating knowledge, life-saving skills, and skills to assist in earning a living.*

**Grihasta** – *the age to settle into a family life and experience the bliss of camaraderie, companionship and material well-being.*

**Vanaprastha** – *the age to withdraw from active life and get into a reflective mode giving up material desire.*

**Sannayasa** – *the final stage of life where one gives up all material desires and devotes oneself to the quest of finding the truth. It is not action-less it is only selfless action and service and penance that mark this stage of life.*

Again the stages of life described above have a universal appeal. It isn't surprising then to see many of the richest and most successful, turning to philanthropic and altruistic activities towards the end of their career or during their retired life. Needless to say that the desires of youth wane with age and different priorities take their place.

*I am no authority on this subject, however it is an effort to share whatever minimal I understood about why Hinduism is said to be 'a way of life' and why it is not a religion but an observation and recognition of human needs through various stages of life. The thoughts presented here are neither sufficient nor exhaustive to capture the complete essence of the subject.*

# Artificial Exigency

## 03 *Monday* Mar 2014

What is intelligence? Are Humans intelligent? If Humans are intelligent how do they create more problems for themselves than solve? If humans are not intelligent then how can they create something that is intelligent? What is Machine intelligence or artificial intelligence? Is Artificial intelligence about machines being made to do some so called intelligent operations or is it about machines developing ability to go beyond what they are programmed to do? Or is Artificial intelligence more about what humans want a machine to do?

So the question is that, can carrying out instructions as per a pre-determined program be called intelligence? Or can a machine perform actions beyond the program? If it does perform task beyond the program then, would we call it intelligence or an error? Infact even perfectly designed primitive machines sometimes do end up doing things that they were not programmed to do, would we say that the machine developed some intelligence of its own?

I guess the core issue is to understand what intelligence actually is? It is only when we define what human intelligence is we could work towards developing a method of simulating it in machines. Intelligence has been a contentious issue as has been the various methods available to measure it. How many forms of intelligence exist? Are all or any of these forms of intelligence decided by genetics? Does intelligence has anything to do with memory and our ability to recall? **Robert Sternberg and Howard Gardner** came up with a list of types of intelligence. While Gardner had a longer list, I present the shorter list provided by **Sternberg**:

- **Analytical Intelligence**: Intelligence that is assessed by intelligence tests.
- **Creative Intelligence**: Intelligence that makes us adapt to novel situations, generating novel ideas
- **Practical Intelligence**: Intelligence that is required for everyday tasks (e.g. street smarts)

Can any of this intelligence be created or developed or improved by exercising free will? Are we stuck with what our genetics dictates? If we are stuck with what genetic dictates then we can't create intelligence we can only use the provided intelligence and we can only use to the extent provisioned.

So with such questions trained on human intelligence, there are similar queries that arise when we talk about artificial intelligence. Which form of intelligence are trying to create in a machine? I guess if it has to be a mix of all the three types. In the past few years we have seen **machines that have demonstrated Analytical Intelligence**, so I guess the real question is whether a machine could develop the other two forms. Would that mean that human can use his human intelligence to create a machine which is programmed for analytical intelligence but the the machine through some process develops a creative intelligence and practical intelligence to be really called intelligent? Or is it more a challenge for human intelligence to understand these two forms of intelligence and come up with code/method to design a machine that can demonstrate those two as well?

Often we hear statements such as 'machines one day would overtake humans' there would be a 'fight between machines and humans in the near future'. How can a machine become more intelligent than what the humans created it to do? For a machine to develop an ability to think it has to be able to decide on its action irrespective of what it has been programmed to do, and the decided action still needs to be an acceptable, identifiable and valid action and not an aberration. So basically that means as explained above that, a machine needs to develop a free will and an ability to think to be truly intelligent beyond what a human has designed it to be. Can a machine develop consciousness too? What circumstances would lead a machine to develop this free will or this ability to think and decide on an appropriate response which it has not been pre-programmed to perform?

Thus for me artificial intelligence, despite few decades of research and application, appears paradoxical. I also fail to understand the fascination towards hoping for a machine that one day would be more intelligent than humans and also behave and be like a human? However as a friend pointed out to me, probably it is man's way to try and ape nature and see if he could do better!

# Unlikely Champion

I am sure all have heard quite a bit about **Western Materialism** and **Eastern Spiritualism**. The progress of the west is often attributed to its materialistic view point. Contrary to this the East has always focused on understanding human nature, looking inwards, treating this external world as false and thus shunning materialism. Western materialism has an inherent belief that human wellbeing and hence happiness is the result of material wellbeing. Pursuit of happiness is suggested to be synonymous to pursuit of materialistic wellbeing. Contrary to this, Eastern Spiritualism has an inherent belief that any happiness drawn from materialism is temporary and true happiness is through detachment and through an inward journey of knowing thyself.

Today, for many reasons, the east has decided to embrace western form of materialism and has moved down that path, hoping for prosperity, peace and ofcourse happiness. Now that people have gone down that path how could we reconcile these two thought processes? Or is any form of reconciliation, a futile effort? This whole reconciliation process has led to a tremendous sense of dissonance within me. I could not place my finger on exactly what was bothering me – but definitely something was. Self-help books after Self-help books promote materialism yet, they draw inspiration from religious scriptures. Strangely though, when one looks towards religious scriptures of the east it leads towards seemingly irreconcilable differences.

Such irreconcilable dissonance, as a theory states, could lead to one of the following three things. Either a permanent alteration of belief, or suppression of any information that could lead to aggravated state of dissonance or lead towards a hope of getting a sufficient incentive to carry on with the dissonance. This human need to resolve dissonance in one of the above ways, has created a situation where there is a shift in the thought process of the younger generation of the east. Infact, any or all of the three situations explained above don't augur well for Eastern Spiritualism. Also the extraneous flaws that have plagued eastern spiritualism also make it difficult to consume for the younger generation. The comfort that western materialism brings, at the very outset, appears to outweigh any tangible benefits that eastern spiritualism has to offer. So, have we heard the death knell for Eastern Spiritualism?

Interestingly, the glimmer of hope almost always comes from unexpected quarters and as odd it may sound, I think, the possibility of revival or survival of eastern spiritualism comes from the materialistic west. While talking about this revival I am in no way indicating towards the thriving presence of many eastern spiritual organizations all across the occident. Nor am I pointing towards the westerners who find their way to spiritual hubs in the east either out of curiosity, adventure or other tangible reasons. I would rather point towards three stalwarts of Western Materialism who, strangely, through their action have demonstrated that eastern spiritualism would continue to survive no matter whether we identify it or give it any new name.

Steve Jobs, Bill Gates, Warren Buffet. Three individuals who came into this world and have definitely changed it from the way they found it. Yet all three demonstrate certain characteristic which echo much of the sentiments embedded in eastern spiritualism. All three in a process of knowing thyself realized what they were good at and dedicated their lives in working on that one idea that they found to be their true calling. The reward that they really hoped for was more work and excellence at work. It was work for work sake, not getting disappointed with failures or getting over joyous about success. Also all three managed to demonstrate a unique detachment with the results or outcome of their efforts. Despite the personal valuation that runs into Billions and billions of dollars, they lead a largely frugal and unaffected life. They continue to strive to give back to society and improve things around them and all of them demonstrate and untiring energy in whatever they decide to focus on. Simple living, high thinking and high level of performance seemed to be their motto for a cause that was much larger than them. They derived happiness from what they did rather than what they could buy.

Have they in this process managed to bridge this gap between Western Materialism and Eastern Spiritualism? While most of us struggle through our mundane lives, have they shown the path towards true happiness through a life of purpose? Or am I reading too much into? The dissonance has by no means disappeared but definitely there is sufficient food for thought here and a possible come back against the materialistic west and a chance to state that your mascots are actually championing our cause? I know not – but I wonder still.